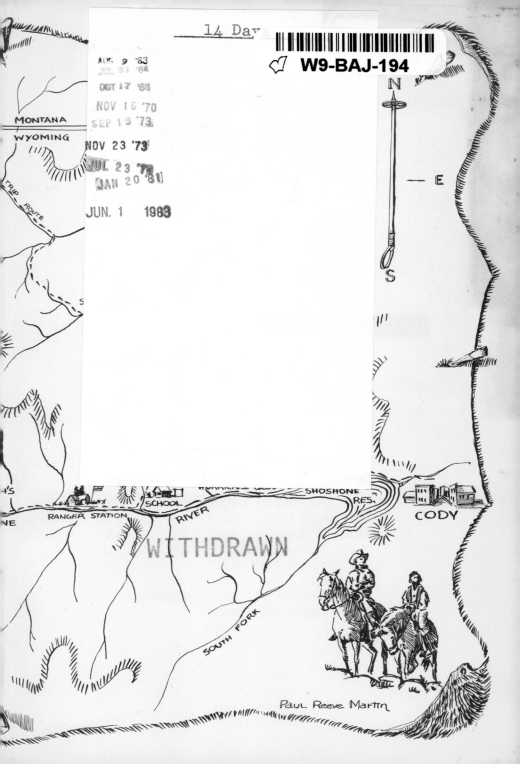

14 Days

MONTANA
WYOMING
TRIP ROUTE

N
E
S

RANGER STATION   SCHOOL   RIVER   SHOSHONE RES.   CODY

SOUTH FORK

Paul Reeve Martin

THE MARTINS
OF
GUNBARREL

First printing September, 1959
Second printing September, 1960

© 1959 BY
THE CAXTON PRINTERS, LTD.
CALDWELL, IDAHO

Library of Congress Catalog Card No. 59-5486

Printed, lithographed, and bound in the United States of America by
The CAXTON PRINTERS, Ltd.
Caldwell, Idaho
91506

To my Friend and Counselor
Professor Bert Hansen
this book is
respectfully dedicated

Table of Contents

8 TABLE OF CONTENTS

List of Illustrations

THE MARTINS
OF
GUNBARREL

CHAPTER I

A Trap Is Sprung

"I AM TOO SHOCKED FOR UTTERANCE BUT I WILL SAY YOU CERTAINLY CAUGHT A MARTIN WITH YOUR CHICKEN WING."

Looking over Earl's shoulder at the message he held, I gave a long sigh of relief. To tell the truth I hadn't the courage to open the yellow envelope myself.

"How like Mother," I thought, "making a joke of the situation, stunned as she must be." I could picture her shocked surprise upon receiving the news that her only daughter had run off and got married to, of all persons, a cowboy!

It had all happened so unexpectedly. After a busy summer working in Yellowstone Park, I had decided to spend a few days at a dude ranch before leaving for home. With no ranch connections, it was only natural, or so I told myself, to remember Earl Martin, the wrangler I had met at a dance at Old Faithful Camp, and to recall his invitation to stop on my way home at the ranch where he was working.

After wrangling horses that summer at Timber Lodge, one of the oldest dude ranches in the Shoshone country, he had stayed on for the fall hunting. I had never known a cowboy before, so every little thing about him interested me. I admired his naturalness and liked his gay Western clothes, so different from the somber hues I was accustomed to seeing men wear. There was something attractive about a man who could sit in company and listen, say little, but follow the talk with his eyes.

One evening after supper, as we sat before the open fire at Timber Lodge, I inquired, "What do you do here in winter, when the tourist season is over and there are no dudes to wrangle?"

"Guess I'll stay on as winterkeeper this year," he replied. "I'll set out trap lines along some of the creeks. It's good fur country."

He explained that "trap line" was a term used to describe a string of traps set at regular intervals along a creek or mountain ridge, and that each species of fur-bearing animal was trapped by a different method.

"Traps for marten—sable to you—aren't even concealed but are set in plain sight on tree stumps or fallen logs," he continued, "with a bright feather or bird's wing suspended from a branch above to attract the small animal's attention."

"Mother has a flock of chickens back home," I suggested, "and if you want me to, I'll write and ask her to save the wings for you. She'll have quite a few saved up by the time you are ready to set out your traps."

He smiled. "That will be swell. I never have enough."

So Mother sent the chicken wings, and that was why we stood reading the telegram that morning—a telegram delivered by mail.

An obliging trapper had packed the mail as far up the river as the Crouches, our nearest neighbors, who

-Paul Reeve Martin

"Traps for marten are set on tree stumps, with a bird's wing suspended from a branch above to attract attention."

lived four miles closer to the post office than we; and
we had snowshoed down to get it. Earl considered
snowshoes slow traveling for the main road, but I
had been on skis only a couple of times; and since
my tumbling technique didn't make for speed, we
decided the "slow" way might, in the end, be faster.

"The last storm blew the line down," Earl said,
"otherwise, this message would have been phoned out
to us." With a trace of humor in his voice, he added,
"That's one advantage of livin' on the forest party
line. You get your telegrams quicker that way."

Even this late in November, the roads were still
open to cars as far as the forest ranger station; but
due to a recent snowstorm, mail had to be relayed by
other means along the remaining twenty-one miles to
Yellowstone Park.

Mountain people are always considerate about the
mail. Seldom did a wayfarer on horseback, sled, or
skis pass the post office without first inquiring about
the upriver mail. It wasn't necessary to call the neighbors about its progress, for I had already learned the
trick, common to those who live in out-of-the-way
places, of "listening in" on mail days, tracing, via the
party line, the mail's slow journey up the river.

We had another reason for webbing our way to
Gunbarrel Creek that winter morning. A circle marked
Thanksgiving Day on our calendar, and the Crouches
had invited us to a turkey dinner with all the trimmings. This was really something special, for aside
from the breakfast bacon, we had eaten nothing but
wild meat all fall. Game was plentiful, so there was
always "meat in the pot," but how our mouths watered
at the prospect of eating anything as gently reared as
a turkey!

There is nothing more exhilarating than stepping out on a frosty morning over the crusted snow, your snowshoes creaking like crickets at every step. As we turned into the lane from our cabin, the sun had not yet scaled the mountains, but its reflection shone on the white peaks above us. A light flurry the night before had left a thin, white coverlet over the old snow and silver-mounted every tree and shrub along the roadside. Except for a prim row of tiny tracks made by a field mouse, the trail our snowshoes left behind us was the only evidence of life on that still morning. As we rounded the bend and turned east on the main road, the sun peeked through and studded the landscape with sparkling diamonds.

"Oh, Earl," I exclaimed. "How lovely. It looks like a glittering Christmas card."

Originating in small trickling springs and melting glaciers on the east slope of Sylvan Pass, and joined on its journey down country by other streams from lower passes, the Shoshone River had worn a channel through the rocks and forests; and Nature's sculptor, erosion, had left many carved specimens of her handiwork in the stone cliffs on either side of the river. In the short distance between home and Gunbarrel Creek there were several of these curious formations—a hen on her nest; a madonna towering above us on her pedestal of granite; an elephant head rising from a little knoll; and spectacular Chimney Rock, reaching over a hundred feet skyward from its base near the road. Although it had stood supported by its frail foundation for centuries, I never approached it without hastening my pace for fear the jar of my footfall might start it toppling down upon us.

The road from Yellowstone Park meandered along

the north bank of the river, now tunneling through thick stands of lodgepole pine and Douglas fir, now chiseled on the side of a steep, rocky cliff, now hugging the margin of the swift mountain stream. One never stepped out upon it without seeing something new, some rock formation not recorded on the road signs.

Because snowshoes made me waddle awkwardly at every step, it was a relief when we came to the turn-off and started up the half-mile lane to the Crouch cabin.

Gunbarrel Lodge followed much the same pattern as the other dude ranches in the upper valley; each log house and group of guest cabins sat on its own creek bank, stitched to a set of log corrals by a running thread of beaten trail. The lane was edged with fir trees and juniper bushes, but every now and then the ranch buildings showed through; and it was good to watch the wood smoke spiraling from the chimney and, as we drew nearer, to see a pot of red geraniums on the whitewashed window sill.

We had scarcely crossed the bridge which spanned Gunbarrel Creek and connected the lane with the yard before the kitchen door opened, and our neighbors stepped out on the porch.

"Hi, folks," Dan called in friendly greeting.

To which Ma added, "I was just telling Dan this morning it was about time the newlyweds paid us a visit."

Then, after the fashion of Western country people, they left the door open to warmth and cheerfulness until we had unstrapped our snowshoes and entered. In the kitchen the big iron stove winked a red eye from behind its isinglass spectacles and gave off the inviting odor of pitchy pine.

Ma Crouch was a thin, middle-aged woman of medium height, her brown hair tinged with grey. She wasn't pretty, but she didn't need beauty to make her attractive, with her easy blend of grace, friendliness, and wit, and fresh eyes that shone with interest.

Her husband Dan was a dyed-in-the-wool Westerner, with a look of caged energy in his stocky figure which made one feel that here was a man who could be depended upon.

"I know you're eager for your mail," Ma Crouch said, handing us the bundle as soon as we had removed our coats. After a score of winters in the wilderness, she understood our excitement. The telegram, of course, commanded our first attention, and I laughed aloud as I read it.

Remembering that the Crouches didn't know about the chicken wings, we explained the joke to them as they pulled out chairs for us beside the glowing cookstove.

This was all Dan needed, and he started right in teasing and never let up all winter. Because it suited his humor, he reversed the situation, making me the catch and Earl the trapper.

"Well, I can't say I ever, in all my trappin' days, caught a 'martin' like this one," he remarked as he looked at me through squinting eyes. "But since the dudes took over this country, nothin' surprises me." To Earl he continued, "Don't tell the little lady I said so, but I don't think her hide will bring much at the fur market. She's prime, and her hair's nice and shiny; but without that orange stripe down her throat, she hasn't got a chance. If I wuz you, I'd cull her out before I sent my pelts in. I doubt if she'd even bring postage."

We could hear something bubbling in the Dutch oven sitting on the back of the stove, and a pleasant odor pervaded the kitchen—but it wasn't turkey. I shot a questioning glance in Earl's direction, and he responded with one of his "mind your own business and don't ask questions" looks. It was then that I noticed the table was set for just two. There was no evidence of festivity anywhere. Perhaps that explains why I didn't burst out with "My, but that turkey smells good" or "I can just taste that pumpkin pie." Naturally Earl didn't say anything, for he seldom spoke out of turn; but I generally kept up a train of conversation—without a terminal.

The talk around the kitchen stove that morning was typical. The people rarely discussed politics or showed much interest in world affairs, and they almost never speculated about what they would do "if——" Money wasn't a popular topic, either, because we seldom spent money. We purchased our winter grub-stake in the fall, and, aside from an occasional mail order, had no reason for spending again until we made our spring exodus.

This was a world of action, so people talked about down-to-earth things. They discussed shared experiences, pointed out the merits of this horse over that, and bemoaned the vagaries of their mutual friend, the weather.

When I was a town dweller, my only concern with the weather had been its relation to the clothes I wore and the house I lived in. Fall meant discarding straw hats and wearing felt; winter meant turning on the furnace and getting warm coats out of storage. Except for unusual storms, things went on much as usual, habits having only to conform to slight seasonal changes.

But weather in the mountains was a horse of a different color, full of tricks and contradictions that refused to be ignored. It was the one thing that never stopped happening, and everything it did affected the mountain man.

The odor from the Dutch oven was growing more tantalizing every moment, so I was relieved when Ma Crouch spoke. "You must have a bowl of bean soup before you start home. It's been brewing ever since breakfast and should be done to a queen's taste by now."

She set two more places, and we pulled up our chairs to the steaming bowls. Still neither of them said a word about the turkey dinner. We ate two bowls of soup followed by wedges of fresh spice cake and cups of fragrant coffee. Ma Crouch was considered the best cook on the river.

After dinner the men pulled out sacks of Bull Durham, and I settled back comfortably, all ears for a story; but they spoke very little as they smoked. I wondered if I would ever get used to their leisurely conversation—the habit of talking all around a subject. They were like sparring partners, brandishing swords but never striking.

Earl finished smoking and rose to his feet, saying, "Much as we'd like to stay, I reckon we'd better eat and run this time. I want to stop and look at some coyote sets along the river on our way back, and we should get home before dark."

We stood for a moment soaking in the heat from the open oven before stepping out on the cold porch. Earl strapped on our snowshoes, and we started down the trail to the main road. Ma Crouch waved good-by

to us from the kitchen door and called, "Don't forget Thanksgiving and that turkey dinner."

In the ecstasy of an isolated honeymoon, we had
completely lost track of time and were two days early!

CHAPTER II

A Savage Meets a Roughneck

ALTHOUGH I was born in a city and raised in a medium-sized town, life in the wilderness was not entirely new to me. For three summers I had been a "savage" in Yellowstone Park. This didn't mean fleshing scalps or chipping arrows; it just meant being employed by the Yellowstone Park Camps Company during the summer tourist season. All of us who worked there were called savages, while guests were referred to as "dudes," We had a lingo all our own in Yellowstone. I was a waitress, a "heaver." One of my roommates made beds and was called a "pillow puncher"; the other helped in the laundry and was a "bubble queen." Other nicknames were equally descriptive: the bellhops were called "pack rats," the dishwashers, "pearl divers," and the bus drivers, "gear jammers." We didn't "spoon" or "neck" in Yellowstone; we went out "rotten logging." We were as proud of our dialect as a Southerner is of his accent and used it at every opportunity. It was almost as provocative as pig Latin.

In addition to our regular duties at Old Faithful, we were required to entertain the dudes in the early evening. The programs consisted of community singing and amateur theatricals or talent shows, and ended with an hour of dancing, during which the savages were encouraged to dance with the dudes in order to make them feel more welcome.

At one of these entertainments, I first saw Earl. From the moment he stepped into the dance hall, my gaze fastened on the lean, serious Westerner in the plaid wool shirt. When our eyes met, I didn't look away as a proper maiden should but smiled pleasantly instead, glad that one of my duties was to be nice to strangers.

Since introductions were not required, I was not surprised when he walked across the dance floor and stopped in front of me to ask, "Could I have this dance?"

He danced well, but made no attempt to open a conversation. Strangely enough, the silence neither bored nor embarrassed me; but when we stopped for an encore, I inquired, "I don't believe I've ever seen you around the camp before. Do you live near the park?"

"Yes, I'm wrangling horses for a dude ranch over east of here. Our outfit's camped about a mile up the road, and I brought some of the dudes over to take in the show and dance. We rode over horseback."

Several times that summer I had seen pack trains jogging along the trails and inquired about them, so I understood the setup. The Howard Eaton Trail, which circled the park, was named for a pioneer dude rancher and was built and maintained to accommodate saddle horses.

"Oh," I exclaimed, "I can't imagine anything more thrilling than seeing Yellowstone Park by horseback. I've hiked along the saddle trails a lot this summer, but one can't get very far in the short time between meals."

The music started again and we danced off for another round. Although he didn't volunteer any more information about himself or show any curiosity about me, he didn't mind being questioned. I learned more about him during the rest of that dance and the next one, which we sat out.

A native of Wyoming, he was born on a ranch near Cheyenne and had earned his way in the world since he was nine years old. His first job was herding Shetland ponies for a dollar a month and his board. In the summer he wrangled dudes or horses on one of the dude ranches in the Shoshone country; in the winter he worked at anything he could find, from cooking in a restaurant to punching cattle. Since all of the young men I knew either went to school or held steady jobs, his life sounded adventurous. I egged him on, eager to hear more about his experiences.

After the dance he introduced me to the other members of the party. One of the dudines (female dudes) wore a beautiful leather riding skirt, trimmed with yards of leather fringe and topped with a jacket to match. I had never seen anything lovelier. They all wore cowboy boots and bright-colored shirts. They made me feel like a swallow in a flock of bluebirds and cardinals.

While we were drinking sodas at the Curio Shop, Earl turned to me and said, "We're laying over in camp tomorrow so the dudes can have a look at the geysers. The horses won't be in use, so I'm wonderin' if you'd like to take a ride when you've finished your work."

Would I like to take a ride!

"Oh, I'd love to," I replied, rising to the bait like a trout to a grey hackle. True, I had been taught to be standoffish where strange young men were concerned, but I couldn't afford to take any chances with a real dude wrangler at stake—plus an honest-to-goodness cow pony.

Lying in bed that night, I realized that he hadn't asked me if I could ride. Thank goodness, that was one thing I could do reasonably well, having been raised near a cavalry post and taught by a polo-playing father.

We heavers had several tricks up our sleeves when we wanted to hurry a meal, and I used them all at lunch the next day. We hated the soup course most. The bowls were big and heavy, and we had to wait for the second cook to dish them up and bring them in. Soup delayed a meal at least fifteen minutes, and what couldn't we do with fifteen minutes!

So, instead of the proper query, "Would you like soup?" we always said, "I don't suppose you want any soup."

Nine times out of ten the answer would be, "No, no soup, thanks."

But because I was in such a hurry to get back to the dormitory and into riding togs, every delaying incident of that meal assumed major proportions.

Each heaver had two tables to serve, and we often reset them as many as four times. That meant we served eighty persons at one meal.

Odd personalities were generally welcomed for they relieved the monotony, but on that day a peculiar couple who ate at my last table, and took their time, were more annoying than entertaining. Plainly the woman wore the pants in that family. Her husband, a shy little man, appeared even more insignificant in the shadow of her enormous frame and enveloping personality.

Addressing the man, I asked, "I don't suppose you

care for soup?" and she answered for him, "No, he doesn't, but I'll take a bowl. I like soup."

I could have killed her!

After the soup course, I inquired about their choice of drinks. Again she responded, "He'll take a glass of milk; I'll have coffee."

When I brought their order—it was quicker to get it myself than to wait for the bus boy—he smiled at me but didn't say anything. I had almost decided he was deaf and dumb when I heard him raise his voice to a mumble and say, "Yes, dear."

After the meal I was looking their way when she shot an imperative glance at him. He dug a nickel from his pocket and laid it down in plain sight beside his water glass. She beamed approval. Had she left me the crown jewels, she couldn't have been more pleased with herself.

When I cleared the table, I found a half dollar under his plate!

I hurriedly reset my tables for dinner before rushing back to the "Cat's Nest," our dormitory. The girls were waiting for me, primed with teasing chatter. "I could never get excited over a cowboy," remarked Eve. "I think those high-heeled boots look positively sissy—and all those bright colors!"

"Well," said Denie, "I saw the guy last night, and I will say he is attractive, in a virile sort of way. But so was the ranger you dated the night before. He really had class."

"Yes, but the ranger didn't have a horse," I answered, as I ran a comb through my hair and jumped into my riding clothes.

"Are you sure it's the horse you are interested in?"

put in Peg. "The fact that you look nice in pants couldn't have anything to do with it, could it?"

"I read a story about an amorous cowboy once, and my advice to you is—don't get off your horse," called Denie as I rushed out the door and down the lane to the main lodge. I slowed to a walk as I approached our meeting place; it wouldn't do to appear overeager.

"I thought you might enjoy a ride to Lone Star Geyser," Earl said, when we met at the hitching rack. "The ranger says it's goin' to play this afternoon, and I think it's the prettiest geyser in the park."

He didn't offer to help me mount. At least he didn't consider me a dude.

The details of that ride were wasted on me. The scenery consisted of the side view of a cowboy, the set of his body as he swayed with the horse, the soft-leather look of his sun-tanned skin. I heard only the creak of leather, the movement of the horses, the low mellow tone of his voice when he spoke.

We stopped several times on the ride and got off our horses to stretch our legs. "You won't be so sore tomorrow if you walk a little now," Earl explained.

Because he didn't talk any more during the ride than he had at the dance, I decided he must be one of those silent Westerners I'd read so much about. Too bad he wasn't staying around camp awhile. It might be fun to get acquainted.

As we returned to Old Faithful, he suggested, "Why don't you go out the East Entrance when you leave the park this fall and stop at Timber Lodge for a while? Chances are you could pick up a job for a few weeks if you want one. The regular help generally quit early in September, which leaves the ranch shorthanded for huntin' season."

I waited for him to turn and wave, but he just rode on

"I'll think about it," I answered.

We said good-by at the hitching rack, and I gave him my home address.

"It's been real nice knowin' you," he said as we shook hands. "I hope our trails cross again sometime."

I stood for a moment watching him as he mounted his horse and rode down the dusty road. He made a striking picture sitting straight and tall in the saddle. It was hard to tell where the horse ended and the rider began, so subtly did their motions blend.

I waited for him to turn and wave, but he just rode on.

As he disappeared around a bend in the trail, leaving only the chink of his horse's hoofs and the jingle of bit and spur behind him, a wave of loneliness swept over me. A lump lodged in my throat, and suddenly I knew our trails *must* cross again—and soon!

CHAPTER III

Demoted

THAT THE YOUNG cowboy from the "land of the Stinking Water" had made a favorable impression was evidenced when October found me comfortably settled in one of the guest houses at Timber Lodge, where I planned to remain for the rest of the hunting season. The day before my arrival, the girl who "did up" the cabins left for school, and I fell heir to her job. At least I was to earn my room and board and a few horseback rides. Would they, I wondered, throw in a cowboy for a bonus?

Commanded by the first frost and egged on by the warm autumn sun, the leaves of the aspen trees along the creeks were slowly turning yellow with the season; and the valley was resplendent in its fall finery. Autumn is the loveliest of all the seasons in the mountains. There is something in the air which defies analysis, not just one thing, but a combination of several: the friendly crackle of dry autumn leaves beneath your horse's feet as you ride along on the soft yellow-padded ground, releasing a sweet, pungent odor as the leaves sponge up into the hoofmarks behind you; the familiar and half-frightening call of a bugling elk; the adventure of stepping into the sun, which still carries a trace of summer in its warm embrace, into the shade where the air is crisp enough to bite; the appetizing odor of frying venison sifting through the flap of the cook tent as you ride past some hunting camp. Autumn catches a pinch of this and a dash of that, blends them perfectly, and then wafts the tantalizing fragrance into the air.

Timber Lodge was located along the banks of a swift mountain stream about a quarter of a mile from the main road, which sauntered on up the valley to Yellowstone Park. Aside from a few tent houses with roofs and sides of lumber, the buildings were constructed of lodgepole pine and appeared very much at home nestled beneath the fir and aspen trees on either side of the creek. Rustic bridges spanned the stream at convenient intervals.

The main lodge was museum-like. Its porches were trimmed with odd-shaped boughs and pine knots; the chairs and benches were handmade from native wood, with seats and backs laced with rawhide to make lounging more comfortable. Each door boasted a latch sawed from elk or deer horn, the tip of an antler hanging from the end of every latchstring.

Water from the creek had been piped to one end of the porch where it trickled out of a big pine knot. Some ingenious whittler had made a dipper from a smaller knot, leaving a length of branch for a handle. Water from this always tasted better than from the more sanitary glass near by.

The living room in the lodge was crammed with hunting trophies, tanned hides, and other Western plunder of particular interest to dudes. A huge fireplace, studded with glittering rocks and pieces of petri-

It was the duty of the horse wrangler to drive the horses to the corrals in time for the morning's ride.

fied wood, dominated one end of the room; another equally as pretentious dispensed comfort to the dining room adjoining. These big rooms were shut off during hunting season, when the days started getting chilly and the nights downright cold. Meals were then served in the "roughneck" dining room next to the kitchen.

Timber Lodge was one of the larger dude ranches; in a true sense it was not a ranch at all, but a mountain resort. It was built on forest land leased from the government and subject to government restrictions. The proprietor owned all the buildings and improvements but was not allowed to fence his pasture or horse range. The string of over one hundred horses was turned out on an area of forest, designated by the ranger, from the middle of June until the middle of October. It was the duty of the horse wrangler to see that they were gathered and brought to the corrals each day in time for the morning ride. Because horses scatter at daybreak, the wranglers often took their bedrolls into the hills at night and stayed near them. With no fences, areas were bounded by ridges, creeks, and meadows.

Once I was invited to go with Earl to find some lost horses, and he disclosed some of the secrets of his trade. By looking at a track he could tell whether it had been made that day, the day before, or a week ago. The trails were covered with horse tracks, and I couldn't see how he would know which ones were made by loose horses and which by horses with riders.

"When you see little piles of manure along the trail," he explained, "you know that they were made by loose horses who always stop to relieve themselves; but when the manure is scattered, you know that the horses were ridden."

Later I was to become, as one dude said, "m-inured" to the subject; but at that time I squeamishly avoided the word, considering it too indelicate to use in mixed company. Earl, noticing how I changed the subject, returned to it mischievously, saying, "I'll have to tell you my favorite manure story."

I squirmed in my saddle, not knowing what to expect, and he continued, "A couple of summers ago I worked for a feller who ran a small outfit down country a piece. His land was cut up, and one of his hay meadows was at least three miles from the home ranch. He had to pass through two other ranches to reach it. Besides running a few cattle and raisin' enough hay to feed 'em, he took in a few Eastern boys as summer boarders; and they paid him for the privilege of helping with the work. One of the dude boys and I were cleaning out the corrals one day and hauling the manure to his lower hay pasture. When we passed through the first ranch, the owner called from the barn, 'Whatcha got there?'

"I waved my free hand and shouted back, 'Oh, a load of manure and a dude.'

"Almost the same conversation was repeated when we passed through the next place. The dude kid was quiet for a spell, and then he turned to me and asked, 'Say, Earl, will you do me a favor?'

" 'Sure thing,' I replied. 'What is it?'

" 'Well,' he continued, 'the next time anybody asks you what you got there, would you mind saying, "A *dude* and a load of manure." ' "

I heaved a sigh of relief.

"When tracking horses," Earl said, "the disposition of an animal has to be considered; and the horses are as different as people. In every herd there are always

one or two who are just plumb ornery—like Hideaway. He's no leader, but I had to make a bell horse
of him anyway."

"A bell horse? What's that?" I interrupted.

"We strap bells around the necks of the horses that
stray away from the herd so they can be traced by
the jingle," he explained. "I reckon just such a critter
as Hideaway is responsible for the expression 'horse
sense'; for when he smells a wrangler, he hunts himself a sheltered pine and hides under it like he was
glued. The old son-of-a-gun, he'll let the deer flies
eat him up rather than swish his tail, for fear he'll
ring his bell.

"There are others who rate bells," he went on. "For
instance, Nosy, the gray mare. The grass across the
crick always looks better than that under her nose,
and soon she's wandered miles away from the others.
The horse I call Troublemaker is my worst problem.
Not satisfied with the grief he himself causes me, he's
forever lurin' some other horse to desert the herd and
take off over the ridge, which means I have to ride an
extra circle to pick 'em both up."

Oh, a horse wrangler has his troubles and calls his
horses a lot of names not mentioned on their bills of
sale.

With a few exceptions, dude-ranch lingo was the
same as that spoken in the park. However, when a
dude stepped across the park boundary, he automatically became a "roughneck." I was proud of the title
"savage," but it took months before I could graciously
respond to the name of roughneck. In my own esti-
mation at least, this term lowered my social standing
several notches.

The roughneck dining room had its fireplace, too;

and after the supper dishes were cleared away, it made a cozy living room. Within the arc of warmth from the blazing fire, we gathered in the evenings, the hunters to discuss the day's adventures with the guide and the ranch family and I to sit wide-eyed, absorbing all the atmosphere I could.

One by one the others retired, leaving Earl and Jeff and me to watch the embers die.

Jeff, one of the older guides, had appointed himself a posse of one to ride herd on Earl. You could tell he was afraid Earl and I would become interested in each other; and he wasn't going to let that happen! Because his own marriage to an Eastern girl hadn't weathered the first winter, he claimed that a roughneck couldn't marry a dude and make it stick.

"East an' West can't mix any more'n oil an' water," he said. "After the new wears off, marriage is only a cocklebur under a gal's saddle; an' she finds herself a-settin' in a bed of cactus cryin' fer mamma, her horse hightailin' it back to the home corral, and her a-wishin' she'd never set foot on Wyoming soil."

Apparently he thought himself an authority on the subject, for he cited numerous cases, none of which had turned out successfully.

Earl didn't offer any argument; and since I knew nothing about the subject, I, too, just sat and listened.

We generally managed to out-sit him, though, and then we moved our chairs closer to the fire and to each other. Earl took a short length of rope from a cubbyhole in the bookcase, and the stage was set for another lesson in knot tying.

He taught me how to tie twelve knots that fall, the most useful of which were the bowline, a nonslip knot used to tie an animal around the neck; the timber hitch, used to snake in logs; the sheepshank, utilized when a rope must be temporarily shortened; and the diamond hitch, which held a pack securely on a mule or horse.

In view of what happened afterwards, we called them "courting knots."

CHAPTER IV

I Hire Out To Be Tough

SEVERAL TIMES it has been my misfortune to be in an intimate group when someone pipes up with "Oh, I'll never forget the night John proposed——" Then off race the narrators, stumbling over each other in their eagerness to relate their own romantic stories, while I remain silent, hoping that nobody will inquire about mine. Strangely enough, neither of us remembers any proposal. We must have had some understanding, however, for when I left the ranch on the first lap of my journey back to Kansas, it was with the intention of returning the following spring to the jingle of wedding bells.

Earl preceded me down country by several days. With the help of another cowboy, he was driving the horses, which had been kept for the fall hunting, to their winter quarters on Monument Hill, fifty miles away. Here they would pasture with the others, taken down several weeks before, until the next dude season.

We said a lingering good-by over by the corral the morning he left and planned our rendezvous for the next May—I with a touch of misgiving that, once I was home and away from the romantic setting, Mother might talk me out of my plans. It was a long time until spring!

That night in town I ate a lonely supper in a little cafe and had returned to my room to decide whether or not to go to a movie when a tap came at my door.

To a traveler in a strange place, there is no sound more interesting than a knock at one's door. An exciting feeling of expectancy swept over me; and in the brief interim between the knock and the response, half a dozen explanations flashed across my mind. However, I was not prepared for the message, "There's a young man waitin' fer you in the lobby, Miss."

Could it be Earl? I wondered wistfully. Of course not, I reasoned, giving my nose a quick pat with the powder puff. He couldn't possibly have reached Monument Hill before this evening, and it would take another day to ride to town. But if it wasn't he, who could it possibly be?

I fairly flew through the long hallway and leapt down the stairs to the first landing, where I slowed to a walk in order to make a more effective entry— just in case.

Turning into the lobby, I could scarcely believe my eyes, for leaning against the desk, glancing calmly over a newspaper, stood Earl, looking quite as though he had grown there from seed.

He smiled pleasantly and said, without excitement, "There's a good show on tonight. Would you like to go with me?"

As we walked down the street to the theater, I was bursting with curiosity; and after giving up the possibility of volunteer information, I inquired, "How on earth did you ever get to town so soon? Did you fly?"

"No," he chuckled. "I told the rancher where we

Leaning against the desk reading a newspaper stood Earl, looking as though he had grown there from seed.

pasture the horses that I had a God-awful toothache
and he'd have to get me to a dentist as soon as possible.
He drove me in in his Ford."

"But you haven't a toothache, really?"

"Never had one in my life," was his answer.

We held hands all through the silent movie. He
watched the film with interest and seemed to be following the thread of the story, but I was conscious
only of his nearness and of the dry, firm hand pressed
around mine.

That night, after the show, we sat visiting in the
little hotel parlor and discovered another trait we shared.
We both made up our minds in a hurry. There was
never to be any hemming and hawing in our family.

Out of a clear sky Earl said, "It's going to be lonesome out at the lodge this winter. Why don't you
give that pioneer instinct you're always talking about
a try and ride back to the hills to keep me company?
We could be married tomorrow evening and be off
the next morning on a horseback honeymoon. I've
heard you say a dozen times you've never had enough
horseback riding. Maybe the forty-mile trip back to
the lodge would take care of that. Of course," he
added hesitantly, "life will be plenty rugged, snowed
in all winter, and you won't see another movie until
spring."

Had I needed persuasion, this remark would have
turned the trick. Had he intended it to? I wondered.

"My goodness," were the only words I could find.
"What do you suppose Mother will say?"

"She won't know about it until it's over," he replied,
"and then it will be too late to say anything."

Suddenly I remembered something I had read in a
novel. "When you get ready to be married," the father
had advised his daughter, "remember that you are the

one who must live with the man; so marry him first and tell your mother afterward."

That's what I'd do! I'd marry Earl first and tell Mother about it when it was too late for her to change my mind for me. Besides, she'd hate all the fuss and feathers of a wedding!

Although we had been acquainted for only a few weeks, I knew Earl well enough not to anticipate an argument in case I refused.

"What will I need in the line of clothes?" I asked in lieu of an answer.

"Well, you'd better get some long underwear and wool socks. You'll need flannel nightgowns with long sleeves, for the nights get plenty cold when the fires die down. Better get a heavy Mackinaw, a stocking cap, and some overshoes. Never can tell about the weather this time of year, so dress warm for the ride to the ranch."

"What? No frills?" I asked, feigning disappointment.

"No, no frills this trip. Remember, you hired out to be tough."

How often was I to recall during that first winter in the wilderness that I had, indeed, hired out to be tough.

Somehow I hadn't expected the decision to be as easy as this. Certainly a matter of such importance should take more discussion; but it was evident that, as far as Earl was concerned, no further talking was necessary. We would be married on the morrow and that was that!

Though outwardly he appeared as calm as ever, I was sure I could feel his heart beat a little faster as we reluctantly parted for the night. But mine sounded like an outboard motor as he whispered, "Good night," and added, "Mrs. Martin."

CHAPTER V

Trousseaus and Nightcaps

I BOUGHT MY TROUSSEAU at a men's clothing store.
The man who waited on me smiled as we discussed
what size the long underwear should be, and I blushed
like a Wyoming sunset when he got out his tape
measure. I'll never know how he guessed, but he
grinned and inquired, "You aren't getting married, by
any chance?"

"Yes, I am," I admitted, glad to tell somebody.

"Anybody around here?"

"Yes, to Earl Martin, a wrangler at Timber Lodge.
Do you know him?"

"Sure, I know Earl. He's one of our customers. Come
on back with me and pick out a blanket for a present."

That was our first wedding present, and we still have
what's left of it in a braided rug.

Oh, yes, I did buy one dress. It was knitted of angora and was, I thought, very pretty and practical.
It turned out to be neither. Every time I bent a joint
it made either an elbow or a seat. Years later, when
we were collecting some old clothes for the Red Cross,
Earl said, "Why don't you stick in that baggy brown
dress. It will be warm for somebody, and it looks

like heck on you." The very idea! Talking that way about my wedding dress! I felt obliged to put on a show of hurt feelings, although secretly I agreed with him. It *did* look like heck on me.

For Earl, getting married was almost like being reincarnated. Besides going to the doctor for a physical examination, he went to the dentist for the first time and had his teeth cleaned. Twenty years later, when he had his first toothache, he remembered that visit and complained, "It was that trip to the dentist that did it. They scrape the enamel so thin they wear a feller's teeth plumb out."

His shopping was almost finished, only shoes and a hat to go, when I met him for a late lunch. He asked me to come with him to select them, and I was appalled when he paid for his hat. Eighteen and a half dollars —and it didn't even hold ten gallons!

"I bought a bargain hat once," he said, "and every time I went out in a fog, it leaked like a sieve."

I soon learned that a cowboy's hat must be made from good material in order to withstand the punishment to which it is exposed. In rainy weather it is his umbrella so it must be firmly woven to shed water. It gives him protection from the hot, midday sun of the mountain country. It is a drinking cup when he thirsts along the trail. Pinching the crown together in his hand, he can dip the brim into the creek and drink from the topside as one does from a saucer. And I learned to like water dipped into a sweaty hat brim. It had a different flavor!

The cowboy uses his hat to haze horses when he works them in the corrals, and many times I have seen it fall to the ground in time to have a horse land on it with all fours. A good Stetson can be plumped back into shape and never show a trace of its misadventure.

"Sometimes I get a cheap hat for dress," Earl said, as the clerk left to wrap his purchase, "but a good work hat is a necessity."

I learned another lesson about cowboy apparel.

When my father purchased a pair of shoes, he named his preference, tried them on for fit, and walked off wearing them. Not Earl! He was as particular as any woman when it came to boots. The way he tried on pair after pair was embarrassing. I was amazed when I saw him in his stocking feet, for his foot was exactly the shape of a cowboy boot.

"An old cowpuncher gave me my first pair of boots. He had them made to order, for I wasn't quite four years old. I was sure a proud kid," he said.

In answer to my question, Earl told me a number of interesting things about cowboy boots.

"Everything about a boot," he explained, "has practical value. Even the stitchin' on the tops isn't just for fancy, as most people think. It stiffens the leather and keeps the tops from floppin' over and creepin' down the legs. The tops are loose on purpose. They're easier to get in and out of than the tight-legged kind. If his horse is skittish and a rider's boot gets hung up in the saddle riggin', he can slip his foot out easy and maybe save himself from a bad accident. The height of a boot is a matter of choice, but most fellers who do a lot of ridin' prefer at least a twelve-inch top—fourteen's better. A higher boot isn't so apt to fill up with twigs and dirt."

"That takes care of everything but the heel," I interrupted. "Why do they build them so high?"

"The high heel's for safety," he answered, "placed at a slant to keep the foot from slippin' through the

stirrups when the rider's horse shies or bucks. The
toe is tapered for the same reason. A narrow-toed boot
has it all over a square-toed type for mounting a snaky
horse. The heel's underslung to throw the weight of
the rider on his arches. It forms a brace against the
stirrup. On long rides a feller doesn't get nearly as
tired as he would with his weight on the ball of his
foot like Easterners ride."

Most of the cowboy marriage trade went to the justice
of the peace, but I wanted to be married by a minister.
My own was the first wedding I had ever attended,
and I was as nervous as an aspen leaf all through the
ceremony. When the minister asked for the ring, I
held out the wrong hand. I could feel the blood rush
up my neck and fan across both cheeks. I stumbled
through the responses; and when the service was over,
Earl had to drag me back several feet in order to kiss
the bride. I can't recall what the rush was about, but
I was in a dreadful hurry to get it over with. Earl
was so composed during the ceremony that I accused
him of having gone through it before.

It was not until after the wedding that either of
us thought about a bridal bouquet. We were to have
no orange blossoms to press and preserve in the family
Bible.

Since Earl's rooming house was purely a cowboy
hostelry, we decided to spend the night at my hotel.
In my flutter before the wedding, I had forgotten to
tell the proprietress about my plans. What was I to
do? In a respectable hotel, I couldn't very well take
a man to my room without explaining to the manager,
and she had long since retired for the night. I had
no idea which room she occupied so I was relieved
when we found the cleaning woman at work in the

hall. She directed us to the manager's room; we tip-
toed up the stairs, and I volunteered to break the news
to her. There was no answer to my timid knock on
the door, so I rapped a little harder. Still no answer.
I was about to knock a third time when a head in a
nightcap popped out of the next door, and an old man
advised, "You'll have to pound harder. She's deaf as
a stone."

So pound harder I did. After what seemed eternity,
she came to the door, opened it a crack, and inquired
in a sleepy voice, "What do you want?"

Another door creaked open, and another head peeked
out. In the next moment the whole hall came to life.
Earl helped a lot—by stepping back into the shadows.

"I just got married," I shouted.

"Buried? Who's buried?" she asked in alarm.

"No, no," I continued in confusion. "I mean I'm
bringing a man to my room."

"A man in your room? Heaven help us! Wait a
minute and I'll get help."

By this time all the doors in the corridor were ajar.
I couldn't stand in the hall forever, booming like a
town crier, so, uninvited, I followed her into the room,
shut the door, and shouted my explanation in her ear.

I could feel eyes peering from every keyhole and
cranny as Earl and I walked down the long hall. When
we had finally negotiated the corridor, I leaned against
the closed door and sighed with relief. Unfortunately,
the mood lasted for only a moment. The door had suddenly become a symbol. I looked at Earl and caught
an amused twinkle in his eye, but I couldn't even smile
back. The dear familiar world I knew and loved was
behind me. I thought longingly of home, but I wasn't
exactly homesick. It went deeper than that. I was

"You'll have to pound harder. She's deaf as a stone"

a baby, awakened in the dark by some unseen disturbance in the night; I was a child weeping in my father's
arms because I had failed an arithmetic test; I was a
girl being comforted by my mother after a quarrel
with my first beau. Now, at the threshold of woman-
hood, I was again in need of comfort, and there was no
one there to give it.

Strangely enough, help came from the source I least
expected. A moment later, I was in Earl's arms and,
of all things, crying like a baby.

CHAPTER VI

Sour-Dough Interlude

As WE HEADED toward Northfork next morning, the sun was shining brightly; and while the colors were the subdued ones of late autumn, there was nothing melancholy about that nut-brown November day. The air was crisp and snappy. We could sense winter about to make her dignified entrance, while the rustle of autumn's red and yellow petticoats could still be heard as she flounced noisily around the corner. Winter sometimes overstayed her welcome, but autumn never remained long enough. Only yesterday goldenrod and rabbit bush had fringed the roadsides with color; the canyon had been splashed with the scarlet and gold of wild rose and currant bushes; the hillsides were spattered with tawny frost-nipped aspens. Today only hints of color remained, rusty browns and copper predominating in trees and shrubs and grasses. The peaks above us were hooded with fresh snow, and some of it had spilled over onto the higher foothills, as white icing drips from a freshly frosted cake.

The canyon, the lake, the river, the mountains—all smiled a welcome as we rode the trail that morning. They know we are their kind of people, I reflected—

that we see beyond their beauty to the need we have of them.

"I'm glad you insisted I have hot cakes instead of just coffee and toast," I said aloud. "This fresh air certainly makes a person hungry."

"Yes, those flapjacks ought to keep us till dinner. I figure on makin' the Harris ranch by noon. A friend of mine is winterkeeper there, and he'll set a couple of extra plates for us."

"Does he expect us?" I asked in surprise.

"No, he doesn't even know I'm married. He'll be surprised when I ride in with a bride."

"Dear me," I said, "we can't drop in at mealtime without giving him any warning, can we?"

"Sure, he'll get even by dropping in on us sometime."

I must have looked the alarm I felt, for he went on, "That'll be something else to get used to, honey. Out here, instead of sayin' 'Hello' when folks drop in unexpected, we always say, 'When did you eat?' "

"Which means, I take it, that you always feed a visitor?"

"Yes, but company don't come often, and when they do, you're so glad to see 'em you wouldn't mind gettin' up at midnight. Mountain folks don't expect any fuss, though. We just stick in an extra potato, put another place at the table, and 'soup's on.' You'll get used to it."

"I'm realizing more every minute how much I'll have to get used to," I replied. "Your way of life is so different from ours back in the Middle West. I hope you won't rue the day you married a 'half-breed.' "

In fun Earl had often called me his "little half-breed" —half dude and half roughneck.

"Let me worry about that. Given time, you'll learn. Besides, I'll always be around to lend a hand."

"I'll always be around"—it was a warming thought. Even on that first morning together, I reflected that there would be many times when success or failure would depend upon his "always being around!"

Earl interrupted my thoughts. "Why so quiet? Don't the prospect of havin' me underfoot for the rest of your life appeal to you?"

"Of course it does." I smiled. "I was just thinking of the hours of preparation it takes to get ready for company back home, and of how simple you make it sound when you say, 'Just stick in an extra potato.'"

As we jogged along, my attention was divided three ways—husband, scenery, and riding skirt.

Before we left town that morning, Earl had said, "We have one more job to do before we head for the hills."

"What's that?"

"Get you a riding skirt. You didn't think I'd let my bride ride home in a pair of baggy knickers like any dude, did you?"

A riding skirt! Surely he didn't mean one of those lovely leather affairs trimmed with fringe! My feet hardly touched the sidewalk as I went with him to the saddle shop. Fifteen minutes later I stepped out wearing the finest buckskin riding skirt I'd ever seen, bar none. To me it was more beautiful than any wedding gown, complete with veil and train.

Earl was right, I thought, as we came to the end of the canyon and turned west on the lake shore—it is as practical as it is beautiful, for it certainly makes a good windbreak.

As we approached the old Thurman place, we saw

smoke curling from the kitchen chimney and Earl said, "Let's get off and stretch our legs and say 'hello' to Hurricane Bill."

Because he had worked as corral boss at Timber Lodge during dude season, I had heard of Hurricane Bill and knew him to be as Western as sagebrush and alkali. He came from Colorado as a young man and worked around the cattle or dude ranches every summer. Like most Westerners of the frontier school, he was close-mouthed about his personal affairs. There were several stories about his past. One said he had quarreled with his sweetheart in Colorado and ridden away. Another hinted that the law had driven him out.

"About his past," Earl said, reading my thoughts, "we don't know or care. To us he's Hurricane Bill, and that's enough. He's a good-hearted old cuss, and, when he's sober, you won't find a better tale-spinner anywhere."

As we dismounted at the hitching rack, a shepherd dog ran out and barked ferociously.

"Don't do that," Earl warned as I reached down to pat him. "Never touch a strange dog. Speak to him and find out if he's friendly before you pat him."

The door opened and Hurricane Bill stepped out and called, "Shep's gentle as a kitten—eats bread from the hand and meat from the leg!"

Bill, a tall, spare man of sixty, made quite a picture as he stood in the doorway. On a face rusted from exposure and lined with open-air wrinkles, he wore a straggling walrus moustache. I could hardly keep my eyes off a pair of the "bowleggedest" legs I'd ever seen. I learned later that one of them had been broken in a fall from a horse and had not been properly set. The tight Levi's he wore only accentuated the bow.

The door opened and Hurricane Bill stepped out

Once I remarked to Earl, "You've spent most of your life in the saddle and yet your legs are straight. How did it happen?"

Indignantly he explained that the popular belief that all cowboys had bowlegs was a fallacy.

"A rider's legs are as straight as a postman's," he defended.

Earl introduced me to Bill, and he twinkled, "I mighta knowed that a feller with a high foretop and a wavy mane, like Earl, would have a rovin' mind to go with 'em."

He invited us into his clean kitchen where sourdough cakes were sizzling on the griddle. They smelled so good and looked so appetizing that we couldn't refuse his invitation to eat another breakfast. As I poured syrup over my third cake, it suddenly struck me funny as I thought, "The only thing we've had to eat since we got married is hot cakes. I wonder if life is to be one long succession of sour doughs?"

I wasn't far off. We were to have hot cakes three hundred and sixty-five days of the year; and when, on the three hundred and sixty-sixth, I served toast, my family was to appear early for dinner, complaining that they couldn't hold out until noon on such a light breakfast.

Those hot cakes eaten on that beautiful November morning in a typical cowboy kitchen were the best I ever tasted. Hospitality was dispensed with an easy grace that any city hostess might well emulate. Bill merely added to the batter as we visited, fixed the table, and invited us to "Come and get it."

When I raved about how good the cakes were, Hurricane Bill looked at me, amusement sparkling in his eyes.

"Don't you know how to make sour doughs, young lady?" he asked.

"No," I admitted, feeling almost illiterate, "but I've watched Mother make waffle batter, and I imagine it's about the same."

"Nope, it ain't," he corrected. "We don't go for them sassiety pancakes with the tire treads on. Plain ol' sour doughs are our dish. You might land a man without knowin' how to make 'em, but you can't hold him lessen you learn how pronto."

"Would you give me the recipe?" I asked eagerly.

"Wal," was his pleased reply, "I don't exactly have no recipe, but I kin tell you how I mix 'em up. You take flour an' water an' make a medium-heavy batter, put in about half a dry yeast cake, an' set it in a warm place until it starts workin' good and lively. When you get ready to make the cakes, take what you need outen the jar, always leavin' enough in to start the next batch. Add salt an' sody an' eggs an' sugar, if you got any eggs—an' mebbe a little more water if it's too thick. Don't use no milk cuz it leaves 'em flat. When there's some dough left, I pour it back in the jar; an' every night I mix more flour an' water in it fer the next mornin'. Nothin' much to it, but I reckon you gotta git the feel of it afore you can get it jest right."

The directions seemed a little vague to me, and I wanted to ask more; but Earl's expression registered "period!" so I refrained. Perhaps he knew how to make them, too, and I could get the details later.

We stayed so long that I began to fidget, thinking of the long ride ahead; but Earl didn't seem to be in any hurry. On the way up the road a little later, I said, "At the rate we're going, we won't be home for a week."

He smiled, but made no comment. We rode the few miles to the Harris ranch where we had planned to have dinner, but we were too full of hot cakes to eat again. After a brief chat, we rode on in comfortable silence, until we turned off the main road at Cannonball Creek and started up the trail to Snoose Mountain. I could contain myself no longer.

"Oh, Earl," I entreated, "we simply can't stop and visit anyone else, or we'll never get home."

"We aren't going home tonight, honey. Did you think I'd let you ride the whole forty miles in one day? You wouldn't sit down for a week. We'll spend the night with the Petersons up on Snoose Mountain."

"Are we just dropping in on them, too?"

"Yes," he answered and, manners or no manners, I was relieved. I was beginning to feel stiff about the knees—and other places. "They run a dude ranch in summer but are in their winter quarters now. They always keep a cabin made up for riders who drop in. I have stayed there many a night and always received a welcome. Fact is, I worked for Hans three summers, wrangling horses for his pack outfit. His wife will be glad to see another woman, since their place is off the beaten trail."

The trail led up and up; the view grew in vastness as we climbed. At several switchbacks, I stopped a minute to "oh" and "ah" at the magnificent scenery.

Earl was amused. "You seem to forget you'll be livin' in these mountains the rest of your life. Everywhere you look in this country you see beauty, and you'll cover plenty of country if you follow in my tracks."

That night I was good and ready to slide between the downy cotton blankets. I looked fondly at the long Mother Hubbard nightgown that had seemed so unromantic and unfashionable the day before.

"Common sense sets the style here," Earl counseled, "and if you don't follow her orders, you'll get 'hell in the neck sideways' every time."

CHAPTER VII

Here Comes the Bride

NEXT MORNING, in that blissful moment between sleeping and waking, we were dully conscious of a disturbance outside, so we were not surprised to wake up to a "spell o' weather." We could hear the fine sleet as it peppered against the roof, while vagrant particles sifted into the cabin through the unfilled cracks around the chimney hole.

Earl got up first and started a fire in our little stove. Standing a small piece of firewood on end, he whittled shavings down from the top with his pocket knife, leaving them anchored to the wood at the bottom. When finished, the whittled end looked like a coarse broom.

"My mother used to call these prayer sticks," he remarked, "but she didn't know where the name came from. I guess because you stick 'em in the stove and pray the fire will go."

Touching a match to one of these, he let it catch well and then stuck it in the stove, piling other wood on top. Soon the stove was panting with heat. He set the water pitcher on the small patch of flat surface between the chimney and the lid so I could enjoy the luxury of washing in warm water.

"Just as well break you in easy," he said.

We were reluctant to leave the cabin; it was so warm and cozy.

As we stepped out into the weather, my thoughts pictured for a brief moment a steam-heated Pullman puffing its way to a honeymoon at Niagara Falls; but the mood changed once I lifted my eyes to the beauty which lay about us and breathed deeply of the cold, sweet air. While we slept, unaware of any change, our dark green and copper world had undergone a transformation. Everything was blanketed in white. I never saw anything so clean and undisturbed.

Ours were the first tracks leading to the cook cabin, but we could tell that our hosts were up because we saw smoke coming from their chimney and smelled the dear familiar odor of—yes, hot cakes.

Following the trail to the road, after a hot breakfast was an adventure. Due to the slick ground, our horses had to pick their ways cautiously; and where the trail led beneath low-hanging fir branches, the fresh snow brushed off onto our faces and down our necks. It was fun, though, until we turned on the main road and felt the full force of the cold west wind coming down the river. From then on, honeymoon or not, the ride was plain punishment. Romance had suddenly turned heel and fled.

The natives often refer to this same wind as a "Shoshone zephyr," but there was nothing gentle about it that morning. It was more like a gale as it charged with fury down the canyon and into the valley below. Unseen, it was proving its presence by bellowing shrieks and sharp lashings which cut through us like knife blades, snatching the breath from our mouths. Each pellet of icy snow felt like a dart piercing my cheeks. The more I shrank into my clothes, the looser they felt. Earl gave me a silk handkerchief to tie around my face, which furnished some protection; but my warm breath and the tears I couldn't hold back soon froze upon it, leaving it stiff and cold.

When Earl said, "We ought to reach the ranger station by noon," I shivered and thought, "By noon! Isn't it noon yet? Freezing to death must be a slow process. By noon it will be too late to thaw me out."

I was numb with cold. It was lucky that Badger, my horse, was gentle because my hands were too stiff to grip the reins, and if he had shied, the two suspended icicles, once called legs, couldn't have gripped the saddle. Could those two numb clods sticking out of my stirrups be my feet? They didn't feel anchored to anything—just two icebergs adrift in a frozen sea.

As we rode on, mile after mile—we had come fourteen since breakfast—the west wind whistled louder and stung harder than ever as it tugged at our clothing. Would it never stop? Finally Earl said, "We're almost there. Soon we can have a cup of hot coffee and a bite to eat. We'll rest awhile and get warmed up for the rest of the trip."

I blessed him for his choice of pronouns. "We" made me feel less of a sissy than "you" would have done. I was too miserable to answer, but the thought of a warm fireside and a hot drink had the desired effect, and I made it to the ranger station without complaint. I certainly must have looked the part of a happy bride! Earl didn't tease me about being a tenderfoot; he didn't remind me that I had hired out to be tough; he didn't even mention my pioneer blood.

We rode eagerly down the lane, but nobody came out to greet us

He just rode on in silence, and, frozen as I was, I was grateful. It wasn't far, but it seemed like ten miles before we finally rounded a turn in the road and came within sight of the old building. It looked like the Promised Land to me. I even stopped shivering and warmed up a little in anticipation. We rode eagerly down the lane, but nobody came out to greet us.

"They probably didn't see us ride in," Earl said. "They spend most of their time in the kitchen." But his words lacked conviction.

He dismounted at the gate and this time helped me get off my horse; I was so numb I couldn't throw my leg over the saddle. I staggered behind him, and he knocked at the kitchen door. I prayed, "Dear God, if somebody doesn't answer that door, I'll die in my tracks. I can't go on another mile. I simply can't."

He knocked again—to no avail. There was no one at home!

Earl tried the door. "The ranger is the only one in the country who locks up when he is away," he apologized, "but you can hardly blame him—the government holds him responsible for everything in the station."

Then he looked dubiously at me and added, "It's ten miles to the next stop. If you're too cold to make it, I'll break in a window and build a fire so we can thaw out."

I was about to say, "Oh, please do!" when suddenly my backbone stiffened. A whip cracked inside me. A voice said, "Look here, you're the same girl who said she could never get enough horseback riding; you're always bragging about how easy it is for you to make adjustments; a dozen times I've heard you say, 'I wish I'd lived fifty years ago; the pioneer life for me!'— and here, at the first snag, you're ready to take your doll rags and go home. If you can't last through the second day of your wedding journey, how on earth do you expect to weather the winter which lies ahead?"

Earl looked surprised when I forced a smile and stammered, "I'm sure I c-c-can m-m-make it the rest of the w-w-w-way. I'm not so very c-c-c-c-cold."

We walked back to the horses; but instead of mounting, we led them up the lane.

"Let's walk a mile or two to warm up," Earl suggested.

For the first quarter of a mile, I pulled a ball and chain at every step; but once my blood started to circulate, my legs felt like legs again, and I stopped feeling sorry for myself.

We were in the forest now, where every few miles the creeks flowed from either side of the canyon and served as mileposts of encouragement to me. When we crossed Clearwater Creek, a definite change in temperature was welcomed.

"It must be getting warmer," I remarked. "The kerchief around my face is thawing out."

"We're passing through the banana belt," Earl explained. "Aside from a few open spots, we won't get much wind from here on."

That was good news! Funny how things look up, once an attitude becomes adjusted to a situation.

We dismounted every few miles after that and walked for long stretches at a time. It felt good to get off, for I was really becoming stiff—and not from cold.

"At least they can't call me a tenderfoot," I said, surprised to have thawed out enough to joke a little.

"No," Earl grinned, "judging from the way you get on and off that horse, I wouldn't say your feet are the tender part!"

It was a surprise when we turned in the lane at Gunbarrel Creek, because our own Timber Lodge was only four miles on up the river.

I thought, "If we get off our horses here and stay awhile, I'll never be able to get on again."

But that was not the plan, for Earl turned to me and said, "We won't ride home tonight. The bunkhouse won't be cleaned up and, tired as you are, I doubt if you could take it. It won't look so bad when you're rested, or at least I hope it won't."

As we crossed the pole bridge over Gunbarrel Creek, the big log cabin stood out in plain view, and, thank heavens, smoke was coming from the chimney.

Ma Crouch, in her kitchen, looked up and saw us coming; and as we rode up to the door it opened in friendliness.

The opening of that kitchen door was like rest after labor, comfort after pain.

"Here comes the bride!" She sang the words merrily as she flipped her skirts and struck a clownish pose.

Here was someone who knew that we were married, thanks to the party line!

Chapter VIII

Home to Our Mountains

WE DIDN'T LEAVE the Crouches' fireside until the sun was well up the next morning. The ride to Timber Lodge was invigorating, and we galloped our horses most of the way.

At the corral, we unsaddled them and rumpled the sweaty patches of hair under their saddle blankets. After removing their bridles, Earl gave each of them a sharp slap on the rump. Off they trotted down the lane to the highway, as jubilant as a couple of boys on the last day of school.

"Why did you do that?" I inquired. "Aren't you afraid they'll get lost?"

"No," he replied, "they'll amble on down country to the ranch where they winter. Maybe it will take only a couple of days, maybe a week or two. I'll keep track of 'em over the telephone. There's lots of feed left along the roadside, so they won't suffer."

The bunkhouse, used as sleeping quarters for the men in summer and as a home for the caretaker in winter, stood protected beneath a grove of fir and lodgepole. Timber Creek rushed past the back door. A small porch sat on the water's edge. In front, the trail meandered up the creek, forming an aisle between two rows of dude cabins and leading to the main lodge. About a hundred yards below were the corrals and saddle shed.

One end of the unpartitioned cabin was used as a kitchen and the other as a combination bed- and sitting room.

To Earl the bunkhouse may not have looked forbidding in the morning light, but to me it was as cheerless as an abandoned railroad shack. I took one sweeping look, swallowed hard, and sagged forlornly on one of the straightbacked chairs by the front door, not trusting my knees to hold me up. It looked altogether hopeless. How could *anybody*, even a pioneer, make a home out of this bare, unattractive room?

An ugly potbellied stove dominated the view. I half expected to see tobacco stains around its door, for it looked like the kind old men sit around and spit at in old-fashioned stores. I learned to hate that stove; and because of its enormous appetite, we christened it "The Glutton."

In the kitchen part, a cookstove, an old Majestic range with a reservoir on one side and a large warming oven on top, stood against the north wall, to the right of the front door as we entered. Against the end wall and beneath a lazy window (so called because it was laid down instead of standing) there was a table for working space. Earl called it a "deal table." In the far corner and next to the back door opposite me, there was a tall dish cupboard. The top served as a shelf on which squatted crocks for staples such as beans and macaroni. Another table occupied the center of the kitchen area and was used for eating. In prepa-

The bunkhouse stood protected beneath a grove of fir and lodgepole

ration for the winter this had been covered with new *black* oilcloth!

The bedroom was just as bad—or worse. It contained a big, iron double bed with good springs but a lumpy mattress—I looked at the depressions in the mattress and decided that Hurricane Bill must have slept in it—an old dresser with the varnish peeled off and most of the drawer handles missing, and a small, plain table, handmade by somebody who had missed his calling.

I looked again, hoping to find some redeeming feature, and my eyes focused on the windows. I hadn't noticed before how tiny they were—and how dirty! Almost no light penetrated their grimy panes; but even if they had been larger and cleaner, no sunlight could have streamed into the room to dispel the gloom, surrounded as the cabin was with high mountains on two sides and tall trees on both ends. There were, of course, no curtains.

A third look revealed the splintered floor in all its ugliness. It had been swept, but it would take more than a broom and mop to make it presentable.

The room didn't boast a single ornament except the proverbial calendar. Even that was masculine—a picture of a man pulling a trout out of Yellowstone Lake.

Sensing my disappointment, Earl diverted my attention to the badly riddled wall around the calendar.

"About ten years ago," he said, "Dan Crouch and Hurricane Bill spent a winter here. Their favorite indoor sport was shooting the date out of the calendar each night with Bill's six-shooter. They claim they didn't miss a day all winter and came out even with the calendar in the spring."

I was looking at the black oilcloth and blurted out

thoughtlessly, "Maybe we should have waited until spring and had a proper wedding. We could use some wedding presents. A few pictures or some gay pottery here and there would do a lot for this room."

Earl didn't answer, and when I looked into his eyes, I saw only hurt there. I was miserable and ashamed.

"How about that pioneer blood?" whispered the voice of conscience. "I'd say a transfusion was in order."

"We can't very well change the furniture around," I began in a weak display of optimism, "for each piece fits the floor space it occupies. I guess we'll have to concentrate on decorating the walls."

Scanning the room, Earl's eyes fell on his bat-winged Angora chaps which he had thrown across a chair back.

"I won't be needing these till spring, so why don't we nail them over the head of the bed, like spread-eagle wings?"

Their black spots against a white background *did* brighten up the dark wall a little.

"This will make a good rug to lay beside our bed," Earl said, as he stepped to the door and gave my new saddle blanket a good shaking. "Cold as the weather was yesterday, it's hardly stained at all. Besides, I always say a little horse smell makes a place more homey."

It was a bright Navajo blanket—a wedding present from Earl. Already, with these few additions, the cabin looked less like the jumping-off place.

At Earl's suggestion we toured the cabins and found a clean, comfortable mattress; a couple of old hickory chairs, one of them a rocker; and a bright red blanket which we used to convert the bed into a couch. On one side of the bedroom window I hung Earl's silver-mounted bridle, and on the other, his spurs. On the only wall space left, Earl put up a shelf; and I hung curtains from it, also salvaged from a dude cabin. This we used for a clothes closet, and we stored our hats and odd-shaped plunder on top.

Late that afternoon Earl cooked our first meal in our new home. I was too deflated to boil water. We had elk steak, hot biscuits, canned corn, raw-fried potatoes, coffee, and canned peaches. As I ate my dinner without appetite, I couldn't help drawing comparisons. This was so different from a young girl's dreams. The lace tablecloth had changed into black oilcloth, the tall lighted tapers into a smoking kerosene lamp. And this silent stranger opposite me. What did I really know about him? He hadn't voiced an opinion since I met him. How could we possibly unearth enough facts, along the limits of Timber Creek, to furnish conversation for a whole winter?

After dinner, which would have been a good one under different circumstances, I scraped the dishes. Earl put the leftover food in bowls and stored them in a cupboard nailed to the wall on the back porch. Then I washed the dishes and he wiped them for me. Thank heavens, our first meal was over!

That night, with the lights out and Earl's arms around me, fear was dispelled for the moment. He went to sleep first and I lay there for what seemed like hours trying to agree with the author who wrote that all it takes to make a home is two people in love, a wood fire, a lighted lamp, and a teakettle singing! Finally I turned over on my side, muttered, "Teakettle, baloney!" and fell asleep, too.

CHAPTER IX

Earl and Virginia and I

HOUSEKEEPING in the wilderness proved to be a strange mixture of challenge and hardship, bringing at times abundant satisfaction.

A genuine affection developed between Virginia, our wood range, and me. She was named after Jack Baker's girl friend. A cowboy associate of Earl's, Jack trapped up one of the creeks between our place and the park; and whenever he got tired of his own cooking, he skied down and spent a night or two with us. He always went first to the telephone and called Virginia, his sweetheart, who lived on a ranch down the river. After a long conversation with her, he would regale us with her accomplishments, and on several occasions he referred to her as a "hot number." He didn't mean to be fresh; it was just his way of saying that she was tops with him.

On Jack's visits, we played solo far into the night. At midnight Earl was sure to suggest a snack, and I'd brew a pot of tea and raid the cookie jar. On one particularly cold night, we stuffed wood into the range until heat waves bulged from its seams. I remarked to

Jack, "That stove reminds me of your girl friend. She's certainly a hot number tonight."

From then on, we called our kitchen range Virginia.

There was no denying Virginia contributed more toward making our cabin a home than any other thing in it. Back from the trap line, Earl always sat down in front of the open oven door, took off his heavy boots and socks, and slipped his feet into the warm house slippers which had been toasting under her all day. These he replaced with his icy boots, which would then be thawed and warmed before another wearing.

One afternoon when Earl came in, weary and cold, and headed straight for Virginia, I remarked, "I never thought I'd live to see the day when I'd play second fiddle to an old wood stove."

Behind the warming oven, on an improvised clothesline, he hung his lumberjack socks, which were wet around the tops from the balls of ice and snow which clung to the wool. Then he stuck his feet far into the oven for a final toasting, while he listened to the cheerful song of the teakettle and breathed the sweet aroma of coffee steaming in the pot. Chances were, Tag-along, our cat, would stretch her nose out from her bed at the end of the stove and purr a welcome.

After that winter I vowed never to be without an old-fashioned range. We have moved several times since, each move taking us a little closer to so-called civilization; but there has always been a Virginia in our home. The new ranges may be foolproof and much easier to keep clean, but we could never warm up to one enough to include it in our family circle, as we do Virginia.

Compared with the crackling, living flame of a wood fire, there is nothing cheerful about her city cousin, the electric range. Beans do not bake slowly all day in its oven; the teakettle isn't forever singing on its breast; a dinner doesn't wait unharmed in its warming oven for a belated diner. It's just a boxlike, sanitary, modern contraption, sans feeling, sans temperament, sans individuality. If we had one, we wouldn't even give it a name. We'd just call it "the stove."

True, Virginia occasionally indulged in a temper tantrum when the wind blew from a certain quarter; and until I learned to cope with her whimsies, it sometimes took a handful of matches to get her off to a good start.

One of our neighbors down country discovered another use for her wood range. She called me up one blustery March day to say, "We're right in the middle of lambing, and I have three bum lambs in the kitchen."

"What's a bum lamb?" I inquired.

"A bum is one that has lost his mother or whose mother won't claim him," she explained. "Ewes often refuse to accept a twin. The larger ranches give the bums away rather than bother raising them on a bottle like I do. I take care of them in the kitchen where my old wood range makes a fairly good substitute for a ewe. One little fellow, who was about to die, is lying rolled up in a blanket on the oven door. I think he may pull through now he's warmed up. Another, a little stronger, has just had his dinner from a bottle and is wrapped up under the stove, where it isn't quite so warm; while a third, which was only chilled, has been fed and put in a box behind. There's something downright maternal about a good old kitchen range."

During the long winter evenings, Virginia's end of the cabin was Earl's workshop. Here, in front of her open-oven hearth, he did his homework. The day's catch of fur, consisting mostly of marten, coyotes, foxes, ermine and an occasional mink, needed skinning, stretching, and fleshing.

To skin an animal, he fastened its hind feet to some stationary object (generally the cabin wall) and slit the backs of both hind legs up to the tail, cut across under the tail and peeled the hide off in a tube shape. This required the utmost care, for any nicks in the skin reduced its value. When Earl picked up the skinned animal to go outside and put it in the trash burner, I said, "Why don't you save it for Tag-along?"

"Oh, he won't touch it," he answered, and I can't say that I blamed the cat. Could anything be more repulsive than a skinned marten?

Earl used three-piece stretchers for his pelts. He made them from half-inch soft lumber, rounding and sanding the two outside pieces to fit the pelt snugly. A center wedge was forced between the others to take up any slack. Hides were placed on these boards, flesh side out. Each type of animal had its own stretcher. Marten and mink measured about two feet long; a fox was approximately three feet long; a coyote was four feet, and an ermine was only twelve to fourteen inches.

The next step was called "fleshing." Every tiny bit of meat and membrane was removed to keep the hide from spoiling. What he couldn't pull or pick off with his fingers, Earl scraped off with a dull knife. The pelts were then put in an airy place to dry thoroughly without artificial heat. They were checked daily so that they wouldn't get too dry and become brittle. When they were removed from the stretchers, they were turned fur side out and combed and brushed until they shone.

They were then stored on rafters away from rodents,

When it wasn't full of wood, it was full of husband

until we sold them in the spring. That year marten were worth fourteen to forty dollars; coyotes brought about ten dollars; mink, seven; foxes around sixteen; and ermine only one and a half dollars.

Another evening chore was waxing skis. When the weather was very cold and the snow packed, a weekly waxing was sufficient; but when the snow softened and dirt blew on it, the skis were waxed every day or two. Again, Virginia shared in the task. Earl built up a hot fire and put the flatirons on to heat; then he melted some beeswax in a can and swabbed it on the bottom of each ski, one end of which was supported by the wood box, the other by the table. When the irons were hot, he would smooth the wax evenly along the length of the skis and stand them in the corner until morning.

Occasionally an evening was spent repairing ski brakes. These were brought into play on uphill grades rather than downhill ones. Earl whittled a groove about an inch wide and two feet long down the middle of each ski. In this, he tacked a narrow strip of elk hide, using the short-haired shank. Down-hill skiing was not affected; but when he went up, the snow sifted between the hairs and kept the skis from slipping backward.

A wood box is another friendly institution. Ours was as high as the stove surface in back, the walls slanted to chair height in front. It stood with its back to the stove and was the most popular easy chair we had. When it wasn't full of wood, it was full of husband. It was Earl's favorite perch when he was waiting for me to get a meal on the table. Heaped with pitchy pine, it filled the room with its woodsy fragrance. It was such a pleasant smell that I saved the pitchiest pieces of stove wood and kept them on top for a "wood box satchet," and once Earl got pitch all over the seat of his pants.

That was the way with so many of my brilliant ideas; when put into practice, they backfired. As Earl put it, "The only thing to be said against your suggestions is that they don't work."

He will never let me forget my first pie.

We had been married several months before I mustered enough courage to tackle pie crust. The recipe book directed, "Keep all ingredients ice cold and cut shortening into the flour with two knives until the mixture looks like coarse cracker crumbs."

I thought it was silly to chop ice and bring it into the house, so I bundled up and took the bowl containing the carefully measured lard and flour to the creek. I chipped out a hollow just big enough to fit the bowl. There I sat, cutting the shortening into the flour, when Earl unexpectedly rounded the bend.

"What, in heaven's name, are you doing out there in the middle of the crick?" he called.

"I'm making pie crust for supper," I answered, with all the confidence of ignorance.

"Well, that's a new one on me," he said. "Frozen pie crust! I always bake mine."

I started to explain, but he couldn't keep a straight face any longer and burst out laughing. My first impulse was to bristle; but suddenly it struck me funny, too, and we laughed until our sides ached.

"Now," Earl said, "come into the kitchen, and I'll show you how to make pie crust."

Using the hot-water method, he had his pie in Virginia's oven within fifteen minutes.

"You're right again," I admitted. "Your way is lots easier."

Mine *was* a little awkward with those fur-lined mittens.

With all her endearing qualities, Virginia did cause friction between Earl and me. For one thing, I was always letting the fire go out. Then, too, while Earl filled the reservoir in the morning, it was my job to keep it filled during the day. I was not very faithful to my duty. How often he dipped into it for wash water, only to find it empty.

Another thing I neglected was the ashes. While the reservoir was empty, the ashpit was always full. I never remembered to clean it regularly. No wonder Virginia refused to heat, and Earl's meal was delayed.

Poor Earl! I must have tried his patience to the breaking point that winter—forgetting to put wood in the stove, forgetting to fill the teakettle before it boiled dry, forgetting to set the sour dough, forgetting to fill the oil lamps before dark. He never said anything, but, in the words of Ma Crouch, he must have "kept up a devil of a thinkin'."

CHAPTER X

It Ain't So Easy

FRIENDS WROTE ME, "I envy you the leisure you must have to rest and read," but it was surprising how little extra time we had. Because days were short, we had to rush to get the chores done in time to run the trap lines. Just the essentials of living took hours each day.

I thought the chores were fun at first, but repetition soon changes a simple task like cleaning lamp chimneys from an experience to a drudgery. Before a month had passed, it irritated me every time Earl turned the lampwick up to smoking stage. One night I complained, "Why must you always turn the wick up so high that it smokes the chimney?"

"When I was a little kid," he answered, "my mother turned down the lamps to save oil; and the house was always dimly lighted. I swore that when I had a home of my own, I'd turn the lights up, even if they did smoke the chimneys."

"Well, I wish you wouldn't. I don't like to clean the sooty old things."

"Oh," was his response, but he went right on doing it.

Running water was another squeaky wheel that got no grease. Earl took exception to that statement.

"What do you mean, no running water?" he would say. "I run in with it; you run out of it; and what we don't use runs past the door. If that isn't running water, I'd like to know what is."

After the lodge was closed for the winter, all the water pipes were drained. From then on we carried water from the creek. When it began to freeze over, Earl kept a hole chopped in the ice. As it flooded and froze again, the hole became deeper and deeper. By midwinter we had to lie on our stomachs to reach a tin cup to the bottom. We dipped up a little at a time and filled the water buckets that way. At first, almost every time Earl came in the door, my mouth automatically opened to announce that the bottom had dropped out of the water bucket. Later, as it grew harder to get, I learned to economize. I finally reached the point where I could take a bath, wash underwear, and mop—all with the same water.

Washing clothes was the chore we disliked most, so we learned to be past masters in the art of soaking. The long underwear was the worst. We both wore it that winter, and a ton of lead has nothing on a suit of long underwear at the saturation point.

The night before washday, Earl filled a tub with water and heated it until it was lukewarm. Then I dipped one garment at a time, soaped it well, and rolled it loosely to soak overnight. In the morning we reheated the water until it was a little too warm for the hands and washed the clothes with a "bachelor's wife"—a tin plunger. In this way only neckbands and cuffs had to be scrubbed on the board. Earl did the heavy wringing; and if the ice on the water hole wasn't too thick, we rinsed them twice. If water was so scarce that we had to melt snow, we wrung them until they

Paul Reeve Martin

We washed the clothes with a "bachelor's wife"

squeaked in protest and gave them only one rinse. In midwinter, drying took forever. The clothes either froze dry on the outside line or were draped over chairs in the cabin, where they became hazards when we moved in the dark.

Wilderness food was an exciting and bewildering adventure. I soon learned that cheese soufflé and prune whip would not satisfy my cowboy husband. Meat, potatoes, and pie were his bill of fare.

Elk was our main meat that winter. I was dismayed when Earl hung up that huge animal. What would I ever do with all that meat! An average elk weighs about four hundred pounds when dressed. But I discovered there are infinite ways to prepare the meat, and you never tire of it, as you do venison, because it tastes more like beef.

We hung the four quarters outside to freeze, leaving the hide on to protect the meat from dirt and drying. The liver, heart, and loins were eaten first, and then the ribs, for they dried out quickly. We liked the ribs cut in serving pieces, covered with sliced onions, and basted often with homemade barbecue sauce. Besides this, Earl taught me another delicious way to serve them. This required a good-sized rectangle of ribs. With the fleshy side down, he split the tissue along the middle of each rib bone so that it could be removed. Over this a sage dressing was spread. Then the meat was rolled like a jelly roll, fastened with wooden skewers (we made ours), and roasted in a medium oven.

Over a period of years we have served every kind of wild meat except rattlesnake and porcupine. I've always wanted to try porcupine, having heard that this is the only food available to people lost in the woods without a gun; but Earl refuses to kill and dress one, so as yet that appetite has not been satisfied.

The most exotic meat dish that ever graced our table was a platter of mountain lion steaks. We had guests for dinner that night, and I planned the steak for a special treat. Earl had consented to let me serve them only if I prepared another meat dish. The lion tasted like young veal, only a little sweeter. Although they all admitted that it was good, only one of the guests ate his full portion. The others nibbled a lace edge around their steaks and filled up on roast elk. It must have been the relationship to Tabby, curled up on a cushion back home.

Whenever a notion to try something different pops up, like roast prairie dog or woodchuck stew, Earl always warns, "Remember your wilderness sausage!" and I refrain.

Can we ever forget that sausage! Against his better judgment and upon my insistence, we tried making sausage from elk and bear meat. My reasoning ran, "Bear is to pork what elk is to beef; so if sausage is made from pork and beef, why wouldn't it be as good made from bear and elk?"

Earl didn't have any argument for that; he just knew it wouldn't taste good—and it didn't. Even the dogs refused to eat it, and it ended ignominiously as coyote bait.

Native hunters killed elk, deer, and bear, which virtually surrounded us, but seldom moose, mountain sheep, or antelope. To do so required special licenses, which were expensive. Besides, there was the cost of packing a hunting outfit into different types of country. Mountain sheep inhabit the highest, roughest peaks;

antelope roam the plains; while moose browse along the creek beds and lake shores.

Even though we didn't kill them, we often ate the meat of these animals. Many out-of-state hunters made their headquarters at the ranch, and what they wanted most was the head of the animal to hang in an office or game room as a trophy. They sometimes shipped the hind quarters home, if the weather was cold enough to freeze the meat; but the guide generally fell heir to the rest of the carcass. Some of it was used for camp meat during the hunting trip, but most of it was brought back by the outfitter, to be eaten or canned by his family.

A young moose is as tender as any other young game, but a dude hunter doesn't pay a hundred dollars for a license to kill a young and undeveloped animal. He wants one with a big head, showing a large spread of antlers and a wide spade—one measuring at least a fraction more than that killed by the sportsman next door. That usually means tough meat. "So tough you can't drive a nail through the gravy" was the way Jim, the one-eyed camp cook, described it.

While getting meat meant only stepping outside and whittling a chunk from the hanging carcass, we had to walk clear to the lodge for other provisions. They were kept in a root cellar under the kitchen. Among the canned goods was a peach box filled with cans of different shapes and sizes—all of them without labels. We had been instructed to use them before the next dude season.

"They get that way from summer pack trips," Earl told me. "The labels wear off with so much handlin' and repackin', so the packer stores the cans away for the use—and amusement—of the winterkeeper."

At least once a week we had a surprise meal. Once I opened a can which should have contained jam, and found pickled onions; I tried again and drew sardines. We changed the menu! Another time I wanted tomatoes for Spanish rice, so I took the can opener with me to the cellar. I gave up after opening three cans of spinach.

These mishaps were sometimes exasperating and sometimes comical. One night we had canned fruit cocktail for dessert. I took a mouthful and choked.

"Earl, don't eat any," I warned. "It's spoiled."

"Spoiled! Hell!" was his reply. "It ain't spoiled. Some dude left it by mistake—it's fruit preserved in brandy."

He ate every bit of it, and that evening I didn't complain about his "eternal silence."

Adjusting our habits to primitive living wasn't half as hard as it sounds. The hard part was getting used to a man who never spoke unless he had something to say!

CHAPTER XI

Old Tex

DESPITE THE FACT that I was very much in love and profoundly interested in the new life, I did at times crave companionship other than Earl's. My content in isolation was due to the fact that other company was not denied me. Our skis or snowshoes could carry us to neighbors; and at least once a week we skied to the Crouches for the mail and often stayed until the next day.

And there was always the pleasure of a visit with Old Tex. It was a panacea for any ill. He had the good manners of one who tries neither to fascinate nor subdue, and a philosophy as refreshing as a breeze over clover. Wit slipped so freely from his tongue that one could scarcely snatch it before it was gone.

Although his cabin was at least a half mile from the road, there was a beaten path to his door. Every rough-neck in the valley was his friend and, in the summer, every dude. Nobody ever passed by Old Tex's turn-out without stopping, or at least wishing that he could, for a cup of coffee and a dose of cheer. I adored him, and I lived for the day when my affection would be returned. To be included in his circle of friends was as important to me as being listed on the social register is to an ambitious matron.

We knew before we knocked what his answer to our greeting would be. Because we liked to hear him, we inquired, the moment the door was opened, "How are you, Tex?"

"Wal," he would drawl, "I ain't mad at nobody, an' I don't hurt no place."

He had been born in the Lone-Star State and had spent his youth working for a big cow outfit in the Panhandle. In the early eighties he came north with a trail herd and liked the mountain country so well that he stayed. Most of his life had been spent around cattle, and he knew cows from A to izzard. Even at the age of seventy, he could have held down a good job as foreman of some cow outfit, for his mind was alert and his body agile enough to do its bidding. I once asked him why he wasn't doing just that. The moment the words were uttered I wanted to recall them, for I imagined that I could detect a faint expression of disappointment behind his eyes, as if he were thinking, "Shucks, she's just another curious dudine, after all." But he answered pleasantly enough, "I've got a good home and a comfortable living. Like the Dutchman, I've got 'lamb in my pocket, money out West, and I'm rich off'; so I figger it ain't horse sense to work hard for something I don't need. I reckon them as can't afford gloves grow callouses."

One day I asked him about Denver in the early days. "Never seen Denver," was his reply.

"Why, Tex, you old liar," Earl put in, "I've heard you tell about your trips to Denver a dozen times."

"That you did," he agreed, "but I never got away

from the stockyards. Turned right around and come back to the ranch where I belonged."

"Didn't you have any curiosity about the city?" I inquired.

"Nope, I never lost nothin' in Denver," he reflected. "Mebbe I was scared I'd bring home ideas about wantin' to be somebody. I never did want to be nobody. Allus earned what I needed and didn't figger on clutterin' up my life with things."

At least once a week Earl skied by Tex's cabin to check the trap line in that direction. I often went along on those days and stopped to visit while Earl continued to the end of the line. On the morning of one of those visits, we awoke to a fresh white world. Snow in the night is always a surprise. One is half-consciously aware of the pitter-patter of rain on the roof, but snow never disturbs the sleep. When you discover the ground covered with new snow in the hush of morning, something special has been added to the day. Its arrival quickens one to activity—paths to be cleared, roofs to be shoveled off, snow ice cream for supper.

It was cold that morning, well below zero. The snow and cold made excellent skiing; so after the morning chores were done, we fairly flew up the road.

We were awed into silence by the beauty which surrounded us. The storm had kindly pulled white blankets over the sleeping hills. Above us soared rocky cliffs, their sides too steep to hold anything but a thin veil, their snow-capped peaks reaching for the sky. Below, the frozen river lay in icy stillness. Here, too, the storm had been gentle, softening ice and stone with a snow-white comforter. Trails leading outward from the road could be identified only by dips in the blanket level. Snow clung like cotton tufts to overhanging branches along the roadside, and every tree stump wore a jaunty white tam-o'-shanter.

As we rounded the bend in the trail leading to the front door of Old Tex's cabin, Earl spoke for the first time in many minutes.

"I don't like the combination," he said, "no smoke coming from the chimney and no tracks between the woodpile and the door. Something's happened to Old Tex."

"Maybe he's out on a trap line," I said, hopefully.

Earl glanced at the woodpile. "Well, maybe," he admitted doubtfully. "Tex always leaves his ax handle pointed in the right direction when he leaves, and it's pointin' up the crick."

He stepped to the cabin door and knocked. Only the dog's plaintive whining answered us and a wave of apprehension swept over me. Would we find Old Tex lying dead in the cabin?

Unbidden, Earl opened the door; and the dog, recognizing us, led us to the bedside. Old Tex lay there in a stupor, moaning with pain.

It was wonderful the way Earl swung into action. He gave Tex a quick check and hurriedly built a fire in the heater. "Gotta get him warm," he said. "You start the cookstove and heat some water."

I poked dry, pitchy wood in the stove and rushed to the creek. As I re-entered the cabin, Earl was standing over Old Tex's bed, quietly calling his name. Tex sat up with a start, groaned, then as quickly fell back. Something had happened to one leg. Both bones below the knee were broken. The pain must have been terrific.

Earl didn't try to take Old Tex's clothes off. He

straightened the leg and held it in place till the room
warmed up. Then I helped him while he split the
pant leg open with his pocketknife and set the leg.
Part of a marten hide stretcher served as a splint, and
strips of dish towels made good bandages. Relief was
almost instantaneous.

"Thank God, that's over!" Tex murmured.

Earl gave him a drink of whisky and, in a few minutes, he was sleeping.

"I think the bones are set okay," Earl said, "but at
his age we don't dare take chances. We'll have to get
him to a doctor."

"But how can we get him to a doctor in his condition?" I asked.

"I'll pull him on a sled as far as Gunbarrel, where
he can rest for the night. He's a tough old rascal, and
I'm sure he can stand the journey. Dan Crouch will
help me get him down to the ranger station in the morning. The doctor can come out and meet us there."

Earl took an ax into a lodgepole thicket behind the
cabin and cut down several poles. These he nailed to
an old pair of skis and fashioned a sled. He padded
the rough poles with elk hide and fastened a rope on
the front.

I bustled around the cabin, packing some things in
a duffel bag and getting a hot meal for us before we
started down the river. When Tex wakened, we shoved
the table against his bed. Remembering how he disliked hot coffee, I cooled it a little for him and was
rewarded when he smiled at me and said, "Jest the
way I like it—all saucered and blowed."

While we were eating, he told us about the accident.

"I wuz on my way home from a short trap line
when it happened," he said. "One of my skis slid under

"I finally got loose an' started draggin' myself to the cabin"

a hidden log. While I was kickin' around tryin' to git untangled. I fell backward over another log. With my toes strapped down, the leg couldn't do nothin' but break. I finally got loose an' started draggin' myself to the cabin. Didn't dare stop and rest fer fear my foot might freeze. Sure lucky I'd banked the fire. The last thing I remember wuz opening the draft."

When we were ready to leave, Earl dragged the sled in beside Tex's bed. We lifted him carefully, mattress and all, and made the transfer without disturbing the injured leg. Earl tacked a large bed tarp over and around the edges of the improvised ambulance to keep him from chilling.

That trip was a nightmare. The going was really slow. With all that weight, the sled sunk deeply into the snow. Pulling it just a short distance made our arms ache. We took turns, but I soon played out, and Earl had to take the rope again before he was rested. The afternoon sun dropped behind the mountains and the way grew colder. With each breath of the sharp air our nostrils stung. We tried not to show our weariness because we knew how much Tex hated being a burden. Never once did he complain.

It took four hours to make the seven miles to Gunbarrel.

Dan and Ma Crouch reacted in typical Western fashion. Not until Old Tex was comfortably settled by the fire in the living room did they ask any questions.

Over Ma's coffee and homemade gingerbread, Old Tex complimented Earl on the way he had handled the situation, giving him full credit for the rescue. I waited for him to tell about my part in the day's adventure, but he didn't even mention my name. This was a real jolt to my ego. I thought of how I had packed in

water, built a fire, cooked dinner, and helped pull the
sled. Evidently nothing I did counted.

It wasn't going to be easy gaining Old Tex's approval.
At the moment it was the one thing I wanted most,
and so help me, I'd get it if it took all winter!

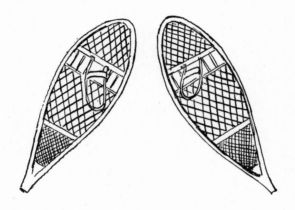

CHAPTER XII

Riding the Trap Line

I SUPPOSED THAT trapping was like catching a mouse —that you set a trap, went about your business, and returned in a given time to claim your catch; so I was surprised to learn that it was really a science.

"All summer while I'm wranglin' horses I keep watchin' for the tracks of fur-bearing animals," Earl said. "I find out where they travel, where they stop for water, and where they den up for the winter. This information comes in handy when I set out my lines in the fall."

He used Number 4 steel traps for coyotes and fox, smaller ones for marten, mink, and ermine. He liked the underspring kind best because no springs stuck out for the animal to step on, they were quicker and more powerful, and they caught the animal high on the leg so it couldn't break loose. The traps were boiled for an hour or two to remove all man and animal scent and then hung up to dry someplace where they wouldn't be handled until he was ready to use them. Because it carries an odor, they were kept free from rust.

Making the scents used to lure the animal to the

trap was the most repulsive experience I'd ever been a party to. The snakes, snails, and puppy dog tails witches cooked in their magic brew were whipped cream compared to some of the ingredients Earl used in his favorite fox and coyote scents. These included urine taken from the bladder of the species of animal to be trapped, rotted manure, gall, spoiled cheese and fish, and rancid lard. One delectable recipe read: "Cut a dead housecat and several mice up into small pieces. Add the fat from a skunk and the scent glands from one skunk and ten muskrats. Allow to rot in the sun, then strain and keep the liquid in a bottle."

I insisted that Earl label the bottles and put them on the highest shelf in a far corner of the cellar, and I never entered the door without counting them, afraid that one of them might blow its top and contaminate the food.

The bulk of our catch was marten, and trapping them required little skill. It was largely a matter of setting the traps where the animals were living and hanging something near by to draw their attention. Trapping a coyote or fox was a different matter.

"A coyote's sense of smell is positively uncanny," Earl said. "The best way to snare him is to place a great temptation for him and then to cover up your tracks so he can't tell that you've been there."

To make a set he turned off the trail and walked with long strides to the spot he had selected. Being careful not to make any more disturbance than necessary, he stood in his tracks and fastened the chain to a stake or toggle, set the trap, and covered it with a piece of oiled paper. Then he sprinkled a thin layer of pine needles or snow over the top of both the trap and the chain, matching the covering to the ground.

He kept a pair of paper-wrapped cotton gloves in his packsack for this purpose. A bait of fresh meat was then placed near the trap in such a position that it was necessary for the animal to walk over the trap to reach the meat. He then sprinkled a few drops of scent near by and backed up in his tracks, covering them with snow as he went.

Even so, we didn't catch very many coyotes in baited settings, as it was less risky for the scheming marauder to kill when he was hungry. The percentage was raised when Earl changed to trail settings. We watched for coyote tracks; and when we saw a number of them following a certain deer trail, Earl set several concealed traps without bait in the trail, using the same precautions as in the other method. He caught lots more in this manner.

A lot of ideas concerning the inhumanity of trapping were dispelled before the winter was over. We never once found a live marten in our traps, and Earl examined them regularly.

"The hides are prime only at freezing temperatures," he defended, "and animals caught in traps freeze before they have time to suffer. Besides, I can't see that it's any more inhuman to trap fur to keep folks warm than it is to shoot big game so some hunter can hang a pair of antlers over his fireplace."

After viewing the many deer carcasses we found along the trap line, I certainly had no objection to trapping coyotes at any season. In sections of the forest where deer are plentiful, a coyote, or prairie wolf, seldom finishes eating an animal, preferring to make a fresh kill when he gets hungry. In this way he is unlike his first cousin, the timber wolf, who will return to his kill until it is eaten.

It took all day to ride the Cougar Creek trap line

Earl set out a number of short lines radiating from our cabin and extending from three to five miles. I often accompanied him on trips over the shorter lines, first on snowshoes and later on skis. At first I was the slave, my skis the master. A thicket of rose briers growing on the far side of a downward turn in the trail always proved my undoing. In an awkward attempt to avoid the brambles and make the turn, I invariably missed and fell down right in the thick of them. Both Earl and I got all scratched up trying to get me out of the tangled stickers. I could tell by the disgusted look on Earl's face that he was losing patience, but he didn't say anything. Sometimes I wished he would, so we could have an argument. It would be better to feel angry than stupid.

It took all day to ride the Cougar Creek trap line, the line where the chicken wings were hung as decoys. When we snowshoed, it was nine long miles up and nine back; but when we used skis, the returning miles shrunk to two or three. When I went along, there were always complications. The first time I tried the trip, we got only halfway when he decided that, at the rate we were progressing, we couldn't possibly make it in one day. We stopped to eat our lunch in a little grove of pines beside the creek.

"We'll start back after we have rested," Earl said, "and I'll come alone tomorrow and finish looking at the traps."

For some reason I had a hunch that he was considering another solution, but I knew the suggestion would have to come from me.

"I have a better idea. Why don't you ski on to the end of the line and I'll wait here until you come back?"

"You wouldn't be afraid?" he asked incredulously.

"Afraid? Of course not!" I answered. "There's nothing to be afraid of, is there?"

"Not a thing," was his reply as he gave me a cherished look of approval. "I'll lay a fire for you, and when you get chilly, you can light it. I'd start one now, but dry wood is scarce, so you'd better save it."

Using the paper wrappers from our sandwiches and kindling dug from a pitchy tree stump, he laid the fire. Then he gathered a big pile of extra wood, strapped on his skis, and was on his way.

As I watched him disappear over the brow of the hill, I was so frightened that it was all I could do to keep from calling him back.

"This is a lot to pay for one short look of approval," I thought. Little did I dream that those infrequent looks would be my only tangible reward for trying so hard to be a good roughneck. Often I hungered to hear him say, just once, "You're doing fine, honey," but he never did. Later, when I was visiting a sick friend, her husband made frequent visits to pat her on the head and tell her that she must hurry and get well because the house was so empty without her. Wistfully, I said, "I wish Earl would show a little sympathy when I am sick. I just lay there and feel sorry for myself."

"I guess we women are never satisfied," she answered. "When you get sick you don't think you get any attention; but you get up to a clean house, the floor's swept, and the dishes washed. I get the lion's share of sympathy and wonderful bedside speeches; but while Al's making them, the dishes pile up in the sink." The memory of her reply has helped me through many similar situations.

I should not have been afraid, for there was nothing there to harm me. It was the stillness that awed—there was nothing to fill it, not even a sigh of the breeze through the pines. I had never been in such a quiet place. Wild solitude surrounded me. There was no sign of life. I felt completely abandoned. Even Earl's ski trail leading over the brow of the hill failed to comfort me in the vast silence.

The sun, sifting down between the branches, was warm; and I was dressed for the weather, so there was no excuse for lighting the fire so soon after Earl left. I did, though, long before I needed it—for company.

There is nothing more sociable than a pinewood fire. Its bright flames bring fellowship, and I hugged its warmth. As the fire crackled and the circle of snow around it receded, my loneliness vanished. While the flames cast pink shadows upon the white world about me, I watched the changing shapes of the embers and became so engrossed that I didn't even see Earl return. I just looked up in surprise to discover him standing there. It was my first lesson in the fascination of forest quietness.

After that I almost always went on the longer trips, advancing a little farther each time and waiting for him beside a campfire. I solved a lot of my problems on those afternoons. The day I made it to the end of the line was a red-letter day. We found a marten in the last trap, and Earl had it mounted as a neckpiece for a present.

The trail was a rough one as it did not follow the creek all the way. Sometimes the banks rose steeply from the frozen water's edge so the path was routed along the sidehill; and other times it cut through the deep forest to pick up the creek at a more favorable

spot. Tributary streams often cut deep coulees across
the trail, and it took considerable manipulation to accommodate one's skis to the unrelenting angles.

One day we were about five miles from home when
we hit the worst spot. Earl glided gracefully down
the side of the coulee, lifting his skis before they slid
under the snowdrift on the other side and walking
briskly up the bank. Close behind him, I slid down,
not so gracefully, failed to lift my skis in time, and
tumbled awkwardly into the deep snow at the bottom
of the coulee. I threshed around in an effort to get
up before he looked back and missed me, but each
attempt only buried me more deeply. In a matter of
seconds he returned to see what had happened, and
I tried again to get up without assistance. He stood
above the coulee, recommending different methods of
procedure. When none of his suggestions worked, he
skied to the bottom and started up again, saying, "Lift
your skis out from under the snow and grab the end
of my ski pole. I'll pull you up."

I grabbed his pole only to have it slide through my
fingers. Down I tumbled, as clumsy as a performing
cub bear. Earl looked his disgust but held his tongue.

I was evidently more tired than I realized, for after
the third sitting I burst out in hysterical giggling. I
must have made a ridiculous picture—a pair of mittens and a pair of skis sticking out of a snowbank,
seemingly unrelated to my half-buried body. Had I
been in Earl's shoes, I would have laughed out loud;
but he was far too disgusted to see the funny side.

"What on earth are you laughing at?" he asked.

I only giggled harder.

He stood for several seconds looking at me, unmistakably annoyed, and finally announced caustically.

"I don't see anything funny. Do you plan to waddle home in that coulee; or are you going to get up, take the end of my pole, and stop this nonsense?"

That was all it took to spur me into action. I stopped laughing as suddenly as I had begun, took off my mittens and stuffed them in my coat pocket, and, enraged, grabbed the end of his ski pole and soared to the top of the bank. Once on top I reached for my mittens and realized that they were the cause of it all. They were so icy that I couldn't get a good grip on the pole.

The rest of the trip was made in a stony silence. I was so angry that all weariness was forgotten; and even the last quarter-mile pull up the hill, which was considered the straw that broke the camel's back, was negotiated without a stop for breath.

If I expected an apology, I was doomed to disappointment, for he made none. I prepared supper in silence, one ear cocked for an abject, "I'm sorry, dear." It was likewise eaten in silence, the stern, cold silence of misunderstanding. My fury was only intensified when I glanced across the table at Earl and saw him eating his supper quite unperturbed, as though it were a common occurrence for us to dine without speaking. He ate as heartily as usual, but I couldn't swallow a bite. So it went until dessert was served. We had canned plums. Sober-faced, but with an impish gleam, Earl ate a spoonful and then looked squarely at me, saying, "These plums need a little sweet'ning; will you pass the sugar, honey?"

It was the "honey" that did it. Honey, indeed! I looked more like formaldehyde! Of course I burst out laughing; and having laughed together, it was impossible to pick up the raveled stitches of our quarrel and knit them up again. Peace was restored—at least for the time being.

We spent a delightful evening, Earl being much more talkative than usual. His behavior that night was my introduction to a situation often repeated in the years to come. He wanted me to know that all was well between us; but being a person who, even in anger, thought before he spoke, he also wanted it understood that he meant exactly what he said and didn't propose to apologize for having said it. I can count on the fingers of one hand the apologies he has made during our marriage. It wasn't because I didn't try to squeeze one out of him, however, for there were times when I virtually sweat blood in an effort to make him say "I'm sorry," at the same time secretly admiring him for refusing to do so when he didn't feel that way.

That evening, matching my mood to his, I cooked a batch of his favorite fudge; and while he stood over the wood box waxing our skis, I stirred the candy and we talked about a lot of things.

I'd heard him mention Johnny Bloom before, but this was the first time he'd ever told in detail about the winter they trapped up Elk Fork.

"It must have been difficult," I said, "living all winter in a one-room log cabin with only one companion and never seeing another living soul. Didn't you ever get in each other's hair?"

"Yes, we did," he admitted, "and once it came darned near breaking up our partnership."

"Tell me about it," I urged.

"I suppose the root of the trouble was really cabin fever," he went on, "but it started from an argument about the right way to stretch a beaver hide."

"Don't you stretch a beaver like you do a coyote?"
I asked.

"No. While most animals are skinned to leave the
hide in a tubular piece and pulled the long way over
wooden stretchers, a beaver is slit down the belly and
stretched flat. While the hide is still damp, it is pulled
into a round shape and nailed to a board. Johnny had
never trapped beaver and argued for the other way.
We both got so hot under the collar that we started
shoutin' at each other. It had just about got to the
hand-and-fist stage when it ended in a silence as charged
with 'lectricity as the silence between a streak of
lightnin' and a blast of thunder. We didn't speak for
over a week."

"Do you mean to say that you didn't speak to each
other for a whole week?" I asked, amazed. It didn't
seem possible. "How did you manage the meals?"

"Oh, that was easy. The one who got up first cooked
his breakfast, washed his dishes, and left to ride his
trap line. The other waited and did the same. At
night we did likewise, and after supper we sat on opposite sides of the stove and fleshed and stretched the day's
catch. We kept wakin' up a little earlier every day,
each hopin' to beat the other one out. Sometimes we'd
have to wait for daylight before hittin' the trail."

"I can't imagine anything worse," I said, "than two
introverts cooped up with cabin fever."

"Oh, it wasn't so bad after the first day, for we
weren't much for talk anyway."

"What finally broke the silence?" I asked.

"Well, one afternoon I got in first and sat down by
the fire to skin out some ermine. I kept listenin' for
Johnny, wondering why he didn't show up. It was
gettin' late and I was beginnin' to worry. Finally I

strapped on my webs—they're better than skis for night travel—and started up the trail. It was almost dark when I reached a fresh snowslide where the trail, runnin' along the mountain under a steep cliff, was buried under fifty feet or more of ice and snow. I was sure scared as I pictured Johnny pinned under the drift. I knew I wouldn't have a chance of getting him out alone.

"Then, in the dusk, I saw somethin' creepin' along the slide. At first I thought it was an animal; then I saw it was a man on all fours, a full pack on his back and a pair of skis balanced on his shoulders. I yelled and Johnny sure sounded relieved when he yelled back.

"I crawled out to meet him, testin' each move before I settled for the next—we were scared the slide would start again. I took his skis and bait sack carefully and we started back. It was sure slow goin', but we made it.

"On the way home Johnny told me what happened. He'd seen the fresh cracks in the snow that morning and had decided to pull all his traps before a slide cut off the line. He had started back but the snow had beat him to the trail and had cut him off. We forgot all about our quarrel and never had any trouble the rest of the winter."

"I've read stories in which the characters had cabin fever," I said, "but I never heard of an actual case before. It sounds awful. I hope we never get it."

"I sure hope not," he replied, and added, "It wouldn't be so hard on me, but it would sure be tough on you, honey. I wouldn't expose myself to the germ if I was you."

That had all the earmarks of a dirty dig, but his

eyes twinkled and I wasn't sure if he was teasing me or chiding me for a wagging tongue. I toyed with the idea of asking but thought better of it. He might tell me, and it wouldn't do to get mad twice in the same day!

CHAPTER XIII

Spring Thaw

ONE MORNING in late March I awoke with a strange nostalgia. I could feel a mysterious something in the air. I could smell it on the soft warm breeze wafting through the open cabin window. I could hear it in the friendly voice of the creek breaking silence after the long, frozen winter. I sat up in bed with a start. This could mean but one thing—spring was here! Spring! Beloved spring!

When I couldn't keep the secret a moment longer, I poked Earl, who was still sleeping soundly.

"Wake up, Earl, wake up! Spring is here!" But he only grunted, rolled over, and went back to sleep.

As I lay there sniffing the familiar fragrance, I thought, "He's too sleepy to understand now, but he'll be as excited as I am when he wakes up and realizes the long winter is over."

I was wrong, though, for even complete awareness didn't quicken his senses to spring as mine were quickened; and I considered him unfeeling when he referred to this beloved season as a "hangover" from winter.

I soon discovered that spring in the mountains is the least attractive time of the year, the earth yielding grudgingly to the changing season. White meringue snow yesterday is scorched pudding today, and tomorrow may be as gooey as leftover gravy. The same beautiful white snow, so soft and powdery and peaceful in winter, becomes wet and plastery and spiteful when spring comes to the mountains.

The cold nights freeze a crust on top of the slush, on which you can walk until the sun comes up. From then to sunset, a step from shadow into shine means falling through to the bottom. You wear yourself out stepping into holes and climbing out of them.

The occasional nice day turns out to be only a teaser; and by the next morning, it will be snowing again. Skis and snowshoes become useless and retire to cabin walls to serve as decorations until the next winter. The bottomless roads make driving out of the question. Riding is out, too, for there isn't any grass to graze a saddle horse and the hay in the barn is all used up. To add insult to injury, the creek gets more roily every day and soon is "too thick to drink and too thin to plow," so we must make the long trek to the spring to get our drinking water.

Earl made his way afoot to the Crouches for the mail once a week; but one trip was enough for me, and I didn't go again until the roads dried up. I missed the visits to Gunbarrel and felt like an exile.

The long quiet evenings didn't help a bit. Sometimes Earl would spend a whole evening without saying anything except to answer my questions. He sat there buttoned up in silence until it was all I could do to keep from screaming—anything to make a noise!

One evening I watched the clock, and for two solid hours he never spoke a word. Infuriated, I finally burst out, "We've been married only four months, and already you've run out of conversation. I must be bad company or you could find something to say."

"Well, what do you want to talk about?"

It didn't help, either, to recall that his silence was one of the things I liked best before we were married.

In desperation I tried to start an argument, but that failed. He never argued because he didn't want to change anyone's opinion any more than he wanted his own changed.

There was nothing to do but resign myself to silence, which I could never do with good grace.

About the only excitement we had during those long weeks was shooting pack rats. The first time Earl slipped his six-shooter under his pillow, I asked in alarm, "Earl, what are you going to do with that gun?"

"A fellow has to be prepared," he answered. "Never can tell when a bear may come along and smell our bacon."

Before he blew out the light, he handed me a flashlight with the request, "You take charge of this. We may need it."

I laid awake for hours after he went to sleep. Every time the logs creaked, I could imagine some wild animal was about to pounce upon us. Finally I dozed off. Sometime in the middle of the night, Earl nudged me and whispered, "Shine your light over on top of the cupboard."

Fearfully I obeyed. There sat a big pack rat exploring the contents of one of the earthen jars. Blinded by the flashlight, he stood as still as a statue while Earl took aim and fired. Then both he and the jar toppled over and fell to the floor. There was no plaster to worry about—it was just another bullet added to the collection already imbedded in the log walls. Perhaps it would furnish material for a story to tell to another bride. Earl chuckled as he pinched my arm and said, "Well, we got our bear that time."

For over a month the telephone was my only contact with the outside world, and I often listened in when Earl wasn't there. My excuse was to get information about the mail, but the real reason was that I was lonesome to hear the voices of other women.

There were no habitual listeners-in on our end of the line. We were all too busy—unless we wanted to find out some specific bit of information—except one old lady who had her phone lowered so she could sit in a rocking chair and hold the receiver. Nobody resented her intrusion, though, for she was a cripple. She once owned a cuckoo clock, but she sold it because it proved a dead giveaway. If people were lonely enough to enjoy hearing a stranger's voice over the telephone, I, for one, didn't begrudge them the pleasure. Party lines were never meant for secrets anyhow.

On one occasion I would have been spared a huff at a neighbor if I hadn't listened in.

This neighbor was a government trapper who lived two miles up the river from us. He was the first man out in the spring, and he went to town oftener than anybody else. He was quick to ask favors but never found time to run errands for any of us, so we didn't ask him unless the need was urgent.

One day I had some important mail to send out, so I called and asked him to stop and pick it up. He said he wouldn't have time to drive in but if I'd leave it in the mailbox, he'd get it in about an hour.

I walked the quarter mile to the mailbox and returned home, not giving the matter another thought.

One old lady had her phone lowered so she could sit in a rocking chair and hold the receiver.

When Earl came in from the river that afternoon, he handed me my letter, which had never been picked up.

Early that evening I heard the trapper's ring come in and hurried to the phone. He was talking to his wife, and I heard him say, "How are you, sweetie pie? Sorry, but I have to meet a hide buyer in the morning, so I'll stay in town overnight. Don't you worry, though; if you need anything, just call Earl. He'll help you out."

When I grumbled about him to Earl, he flatly stated, "You had no business listening in."

The park ranger's wife, who lived eleven miles above us, was even more lonely than I. During the spring thaw she went for over a month without her mail. Several times she called to ask me to thumb through it and tell her what the postmarks were, and once she asked me to read her mother's letter over the phone.

Spring in April was no better than spring in March, but I wasn't looking forward to May. I had been persuaded to take in some boarders who might stay for several weeks. Cooking for us was such a problem that I wondered what I would do with four lumberjacks who would probably eat enormous meals three times a day.

Timber Lodge operated a small sawmill across the river, and every spring they hired a crew to get out the logs. The men slept in a dude cabin but had no place to eat except with us. Only Earl's promise to help saved me from going into a complete tail spin. I had read stories about lumber camps, and always the workmen were depicted as immense eaters, often consuming as much as half a pie at one meal. Well, that was one thing they wouldn't get at my table. Pies, according to my geometry, were meant to be cut in six pieces; and so help me, that's how I'd cut 'em!

One morning, when these thoughts were dragging me lower than the creek bed, Earl suggested, "Why don't you stop fretting and think of something pleasant for a change?"

"Pleasant?" I replied. "I can't think of anything pleasant at the moment. Can you?"

"Why, yes, as a matter of fact, I can. Last time I got the mail, I was told that the neighbors plan to give a dance in our honor at the schoolhouse as soon as the roads dry up."

"A dance for us? How wonderful! Why didn't you tell me before?" A dozen thoughts popped into my head. What would I wear? What kind of music would they have? Where would they find enough women for a dance? What if I had forgotten how! How nice it would be to get in a corner and jabber with my own sex again.

The news was as promising as a rainbow. Before I knew it, the boarders had arrived; and they weren't half as bad as I expected. The foreman of the crew was a fine young man who later became a good friend of ours, and two of the other loggers were young, well-mannered fellows with normal capacities. Jake, the fourth, was the joker in the deal. He was a big, burly Swede whom I instinctively disliked, with a gruff, out-spoken manner and an enormous appetite. Behind his back we called him Paul Bunyan.

Earl did most of the cooking during that first week. I couldn't adjust my recipes for two to so great a need. They ate more potatoes at one meal than we did in a week. It was not until Earl joined the woods crew that I took over. I was patting myself on the back when

Jake announced one morning, "You're gonna hev company one of these days, Missus. My old lady an' our kid, Ole—he's five—is figgerin' on comin' up over Sunday sometime while I'm here."

I must have looked my consternation, for he added almost in the same breath, "The old lady kin help you with the cookin'. That's where I met her, cookin' in a lumber camp up in Minnesoty."

"You'll be sure to let me know a few days before they come, won't you?"

"Yeah," he answered. "I'll sure tell you when I hear they're comin'."

It was hard enough entertaining friends in such cramped quarters, let alone a stranger whose husband I already disliked. From then I was in a tizzy, and even thinking about the dance couldn't divert my thoughts from the impending visit of Jake's wife and their kid, Ole. What would she be like? Would she criticize my cooking? How would I entertain her all day?

The very next Saturday, it happened. I heard an unfamiliar chugging climb the hill to the saddle shed. A large woman and a small boy stepped from a car which must have been here when Columbus landed. I saw her take him roughly by the hand and jerk him up beside her. When I realized that this was Jake's family, I ducked back into the cabin, chucked my dirty apron into the clothesbag, and donned my proper unconcern just in time to answer her knock.

I hadn't expected Jake's wife to be a beauty, but I was scarcely prepared for what I saw. She was a huge woman, weighing, as Earl put it, "two pounds less than a horse." A protruding jaw stuck out like a basket from under a cobweb mustache. A low forehead was crowned with a mop of fuzzy, hennaed hair. She looked as hard as poured concrete. I couldn't help comparing her to the woman who, after asking directions to the beauty shop, found herself entering the door of the local taxidermist.

She smiled, displaying a row of teeth so white and even that they fascinated me. They seemed so out of place. All during her visit I tried not to stare at those teeth, but they drew my eyes as a magnet does steel. Never in my life had I seen such a perfect pair of china clippers.

I asked her to be seated in the only rocking chair, while I sat on the bed racking my brain for some subject of mutual interest. However, she and her son kept up such a steady flow of argument that I soon gave up and began thinking of supper. Apple pie was on the menu and I had mixed the pie dough and stewed the dried apples that morning. But there was enough for only one pie.

"How does one go about stretching a pie?" I wondered, and that made me think of Daddy Nelson, head cook at the lodge during dude season. Once, when unexpected guests came for dinner, a new waitress ran to him and inquired, "Whatever shall we do? If one more guest comes for dinner, the pie won't go around!"

He grinned and said, "Go look on the top shelf of the storeroom, and bring me the pie stretcher. We'll fix that." And she actually tried to find it!

I didn't have a pie stretcher either, but I did have extra dough. I decided to make a custard pie, and they could have a choice for supper. With that tentative plan, I said to the guests, "Maybe you'd like to go to your cabin and get your things unpacked before supper. The beds are made up in the first tent house and the fire's laid."

"Oh, we'd as soon stay here and help you git the supper," she replied, as she plunked herself down at the end of the table, blocking my way to the supply cupboard. In the meantime Ole was amusing himself by removing the wood from the wood box, stick by stick, and dumping it between me and the front door. I started to object, but she interrupted with, "Oh, let him be. While he's doin' that he's givin' me a rest, the little brat."

Well, that was one thing we agreed upon—she had him in the right category.

I wiggled like a contortionist reaching in the cupboard for supplies, but she didn't budge an inch. I died a thousand deaths as I closed the oven door on my pies, and she remarked, "Well, that's a new one on me, bakin' apple pie without no crust an' puttin' a crust on the custard."

If my life had depended upon it I couldn't have opened that oven door and corrected my mistake.

"Yes, we like them that way," I stammered as I filled the dishpan with potatoes to pare.

"She may offer to peel them," I thought, "and that will draw her eagle eyes away from me as I finish supper." She didn't. She just sat there, sticking in little disturbing remarks such as, "You waste a lot of spuds peelin' them so thick," and "Lucky you don't have a big crew to feed. It'd take you all day just to peel the spuds." I was getting weaker every moment. How could I possibly get the meal on the table, I wondered, as I continued peeling, peeling, peeling. She finally broke the spell with, "My Gawd, woman, that's

an awful lot of spuds fer one meal, ain't it? Don't you
figger on havin' nothin' else?"

I looked at the pyramid of potatoes, a water bucket
almost half full, and realized that I had peeled enough
for three meals.

"Yes," I mumbled in confusion, "I always peel enough
for the next day. It saves water."

"Oh," was her only comment as I took out enough
for supper and shoved the pail back on the shelf below
the work table.

I finally got the supper on the table and she told
me, reluctantly, that it was a good meal—for a beginner.
At least we had enough potatoes, and Ole, who couldn't
decide which kind he wanted, got two pieces of pie.
To my surprise she helped with the dishes but com-
mented constantly on the poor arrangement of my
working space.

Realizing that I had had enough for one day, Earl
took over after the dishes were washed.

"We go to bed early around here when we are working; so I'll take you to your cabin now, and you can
get settled for the night."

The moment the door closed, I collapsed on the bed
to enjoy a moment of tranquility. I could hear voices
arguing outside but didn't even try to listen. Let them
fight it out with Earl. I had won the first round.

Almost an hour later he came in, the picture of disgust.

"If I had a blankety-blank kid like that," he exploded, "I'd tie a rock around his neck and drop him
in the river—and throw his mother in after him."

"My goodness, what's the little darling done now?"
I asked.

"He set up such a howl to sleep in one of the cabins

with a fireplace that we finally ended up by putting a bed in Number 5. They decided to sleep three in a bed. I hope they freeze to death. You can throw a cat through those chink holes."

Our bed felt so good that night that I said to Earl, "I feel like staying awake all night so this peace will last a little longer. It's going to be tough facing that barrage in the morning."

"Maybe they'll be in a better mood after a good night's rest."

Although we generally slept later on Sunday morning, something told us to get up at the usual time. It was lucky we did, because we were scarcely dressed when the family appeared at the cabin door, all three of them talking at once. The exhibition of the night before was an amateur rehearsal of the stellar performance they staged while I was getting breakfast.

We gathered that the bed had fallen down during the night, and Jake had refused to get up in the cold and fix it, preferring to spend the rest of the night on the floor with the weight of the other two pushed against him. At least he had most of the covers.

Aside from frequent "don'ts" directed Ole's way, the wife was silent while they ate breakfast, alternating mouthfuls of hot cakes and fried eggs with glares at her husband, who seemed utterly cowed by her presence. If her face fascinated me when she was in good humor, it hypnotized me in a bad one. My eyes insisted upon returning to that mouthful of matched pearls. Once she caught me staring and popped, "See anything green?"

When breakfast was over, she announced that she and Ole were going home. I was so relieved and so afraid that she might change her mind that I didn't

say a word. She left Ole with me while she went to
gather her things from the cabin; and as she shut the
door behind her, he stuck out his tongue and called,
"You old black gut, you."

As they bundled up for the cold drive back to town,
I walked with her to the door and made a last effort
to be polite.

"I'm glad to have met you, Mrs. Nelson. Perhaps
you'll come again, when the weather gets warmer."

This launched her on a tirade which left me speechless.

"Come again?" she shouted, her teeth flashing. "Indeed, I won't come again. I hope I never set eyes on
the lot of you again; and that means you, too, Jake.
And me thinkin' I was gonna have such a nice vacation.
Vacation, hell!" With that she flounced to the car,
dragging Ole behind her.

I stepped back into the cabin, threw myself on the
bed, and wept bucketfuls. Earl stood there watching
me, offering no consolation. I sobbed on, wanting him
to put his arms around me and tell me how maligned
I had been; but silence was his only answer to my
tears. Finally I looked up and blubbered, "Oh, Earl,
how could she be so mean when I tried so hard to be
nice to her?"

He looked at me and answered, "Well, you had it
comin', honey. What made you say you were glad
you met her and invite her to come again when you
didn't mean a word of it?"

"Darn it, anyway," I thought as I buried my face
deeper into the pillow, "I'm not getting anywhere at
all—and I did it all just to please him!"

CHAPTER XIV

Swing That Heifer

PREPARATIONS FOR the coming dance soon drowned out the memory of that hapless weekend, and I began counting the days. Being presented at court couldn't have been been more exciting.

"Now don't get your heart set on anything fancy," Earl warned. "Schoolhouse dances aren't like military balls. They're just old-fashioned hoedowns." But nothing he could say dulled the keen edge of anticipation, for this was something to look forward to and set the days aglow.

The first sunshiny day I dug into our dark, improvised clothes closet and brought out our Sunday-go-to-meeting clothes to hang them on the line to air.

What a long time to go without dressing up! Too long, really. Perhaps we wouldn't even know how to act when we got back into circulation.

As I lifted the box containing Earl's new boots and my wedding pumps, I noticed a hole gnawed into its side; and sniffing the unmistakable odor of pack rat, I wasn't startled to find my slippers full of macaroni, beans, bits of pine cone, and several shiny buttons.

"To a pack rat, fair exchange is no robbery," Earl

had told me. "Whenever a pack rat takes anything, he always leaves something in its place. That's why they're sometimes called trade rats."

But his pilfering made me see red. I could picture Earl's fury when he learned that a big hole was chewed in the instep of one of his boots, a ragged hole as big as a dollar. And that wasn't all. When I hung my one and only tweed suit on the line, I found another hole, a hole too big to be mended without spoiling the appearance of the garment. That tweed suit was my pride and joy, and look at it now! The heck with this country anyway! I sat forlornly on the edge of the bed with the jacket crumpled on my lap, recalling the time when, two winters before, Mother had purchased the length of genuine English tweed from a peddler and of how deliciously sinful I felt when I learned that the bargain price of the cloth was due to its having been smuggled. I remembered the sacrifice of a whole month's allowance to have it tailor-made. Well, it was ruined now—and I had expected it to last for years and years. A nice mess we were in, Earl with only one boot and I without a jacket.

Even while I refused to admit a feeling of guilt, the voice of conscience was saying:

"Maybe you can be excused this time for allowing this to happen, never having lived with pack rats before; but look out for next year! If you hope to hold up your end of this frontier marriage, there will have to be some changes made."

"Dear me," I thought out loud, "who would ever have guessed that marrying a cowboy would entail so many strange obligations."

Earl did not, however, react as I expected. While

I stormed and raved about my suit, he only shrugged his shoulders.

"Well, I hope it was the same pack rat we shot the other night."

On Saturday I got supper a little earlier than usual; and Jake, heaping coals of fire on my head, volunteered to wash the dishes after we left. Joe, the foreman, had already offered to drive us down to Gunbarrel in his wagon; from there we would go the rest of the way in the Crouches' car. Because the road was so riddled with chuckholes after the spring thaw, we bumped along like a hayrack over a corduroy road, and it took us two hours to drive the twenty-five miles to the schoolhouse.

The windows of the schoolhouse were all lighted up when we entered the yard, and we saw several saddle horses and a team tethered to the hitching rack out-side. Some cars, most of them Model T Fords, were parked every whichway in the school yard.

As we entered the door, eyes were focused upon me from every direction; and I was as embarrassed as if I had been caught looking at myself in a mirror. A procession of humiliating possibilities trooped across my mind. Did my petticoat show? Were the seams of my stockings straight? Did my broad, self-conscious grin in any way resemble the friendly, sincere smile I had rehearsed over the dishpan? Oh, dear, this was awful!

The building, used for school, for church services, and for community projects, consisted of a small hall-way, two cloak closets, and a large schoolroom. The writing surfaces of the desks had been pushed back against the walls, the seats facing the dance floor. I discovered, after sitting down without looking, that many of the bundles of clothing lying on the seats contained sleeping babies. Most of the small fry were playing tag in the middle of the floor, weaving in and out among the dancers.

Near the teacher's desk stood an upright piano, around which the three-piece orchestra was seated. Music was furnished by a man and his two sons, all of whom batched on a ranch near by. The father played the air on the fiddle, with one of the boys strumming a steel guitar and the other chording on the piano. Men outnumbered the women three to one. While there were several single cowboys present, the school marm was the only unmarried woman; and she was unmistakably the belle of the ball. A few of the women had on sweaters and skirts like I was wearing, but most of them were clad in freshly starched house dresses. Only a couple of men wore suits; the rest were dressed in Levi's and bright shirts.

Around the waists of several of the cowboys, bright sashes were looped—similar to the one Earl had insisted upon wearing and which I considered gaudy. Almost all the men wore high-heeled cowboy boots.

One man in particular caught my fancy. He was dressed in soft buckskin; and as he whisked by me on the dance floor, I sniffed the tangy odor of wood smoke coming from his Indian-tanned garments. There was a look of mystery about him as he stood straight and tall, bright, confident eyes shining from the poker-faced mask which was his face.

"Who is that handsome man in the buckskin shirt?" I asked Earl, when we had danced beyond earshot. "He doesn't look like a cowboy—more like a frontiersman of an earlier day. He's really romantic-looking."

"Yes, he's the romantic type, all right," Earl answered, "silent and mysterious. Don't get any ideas, though," he added teasingly. "He's married and, as far as I know, has never had an eye for any other woman than his wife. He's our local moonshiner."

"Oh, how exciting," I said, thrilled to see in the flesh a river character I'd heard Old Tex speak of so many times. After one good look at him, I could understand why he had been so successful in outwitting the law.

As I was raised in a prohibition state, my conception of a moonshiner was an uncouth, dirty, immoral person, a far cry from this good-looking man who smelled like campfires and looked like Daniel Boone.

"Nobody fools around with Seth," Earl said. "I've never seen him in a fight, but judging from his aim when he shoots an elk, I'd as soon stay on good terms. Making whisky isn't a moral issue with him. It's a business."

While some of the neighbors disapproved of his vocation, they all respected him; and his occupation in no way lowered his social standing in the community. Never having associated with a bootlegger before, it was no wonder I was impressed.

Meeting these people, who had previously been distinguished only by their telephone voices, was an exciting experience; and, surprisingly, most of my impressions turned out to be correct. Deprived of movies, daily papers, and other artificial stimuli, people in hibernation often improvise; so that winter I had made a game of drawing imaginary pictures of the owners of the voices heard over the party line. A certain inflection indicated a raised eyebrow; a sour note, a turned-down mouth; an animated tone, a pair of sparkling eyes.

Between dances, the women gathered in little groups

exchanging tidbits of neighborhood gossip; but every time I joined a group, the conversation turned about-face and ended in a discussion of the weather. I was sick of the weather and wanted nothing more than to discuss in intimacy what Mrs. Baker said to Mrs. Ames when the latter's sheep dog killed the former's turkey hen. After living a long winter and a longer spring under conditions even more primitive than they had, it did seem that I should be included in the chitchat which made up a mountain neighborhood. I hadn't heard a bit of gossip all winter and was starved for it. Even complete silence could not have been more exclusive than their refusal to discuss personalities with me. There was no getting around it; they still considered me an outsider, and how that did hurt!

Yet what a good time everybody had at that dance! Some of the steps, including the waltz, foxtrot, and circle two-step (which we called a Paul Jones back home) were familiar; but the quadrilles or square dances were the most popular. Since I had never danced one before I had to rely on my partner to push me where I was supposed to go.

Every other dance that night was a quadrille, and no calls were repeated. Square dances turned out to be a lot more fun than round ones, even though they did require more attention and skill; but until I learned the trick of skipping to the rhythm of the music, a quadrille certainly left me breathless.

The calls themselves were catchy and interesting to a newcomer—and sometimes anything but flattering. In one figure, as the caller sang out "Swing Grandma," a man grabbed me and swung me around and around, releasing me to swing the next girl in the set when the caller added, "Now swing Ma." Then, as he swung the last girl, the quatrain ended with "Now that gal from Arkansaw."

I was pleased to recognize the caller as our friend Hurricane Bill, whom we had not seen since we stopped to eat sour doughs with him the day after our wedding. He added color to the scene as he leaned against the side of the piano with his "heels a-rockin' and his toes a-tappin'," adding two lines of banter to one of direction. He never called a dance the same way twice and often spiced the calls by linking some dancer's name with a silly jingle around a bit of local gossip. It was customary, when instructions were brief and the other three couples had only to repeat the figure performed by the head couple, for the caller to fill the gap by chanting or singing anything that popped into his head, adding the gaiety of words to the delight of action.

Later in the evening, another caller, who gave only the directions, took over; and while his calls were easier to follow, much of the charm and savor of the dance was lost. Hurricane Bill followed the figure of the dance as he called and achieved some remarkable effects. He had just started a square which began, "Rope your cow and brand your calf," when I happened to look up in time to catch a twinkle in his eye as he chanted, "Swing that heifer fer an hour an' a half." As we executed the allemande left around the circle, he continued, "Here she comes with the old mess wagon; hind wheel broke an' the axle draggin'." When we met our partners again, he was saying, "Meet your honey and pat her on the head; if she don't like biscuits, feed her corn bread." The dance finally ended with the command, "P-r-o-menade you know where and I don't care, an' sit your honey in a rockin' chair."

As the evening advanced and he imbibed more freely

"Swing that heifer fer an hour an' a half"

of the local moonshine, his calls grew bolder; and I drew a quick breath when he introduced one dance by chanting, "Get in your places and straighten up your faces; loosen up your belly bands and tighten up your traces."

Before Bill became so inebriated that it was necessary for some of the men to walk him around the schoolhouse, we danced a waltz together—and I was treated to a new sensation. The tune "Over the Waves" could not have been more appropriate. Due to the "hitch in his get-along," one step carried us to the crest of the wave and the next to the trough, the moonshine he had consumed only added to the turbulence of the waters.

I had the next dance with Earl, and he scolded me.

"You don't have to dance with him when he is tight. None of the other women do. Tell him you've got the dance with me."

"Oh, it wasn't so bad," I answered, "and if you think he's tight, try dancing with him. I'd say he's more inclined toward looseness."

At midnight, lunch was announced and everybody scurried to a seat, while a big box of tin cups was passed around. A cowboy followed and filled them with steaming coffee poured from a big camp coffeepot. The women brought homemade cakes and sandwiches, which were passed again and again. Sick and tired of my own cooking, I ate like a horse.

Immediately after lunch, there was a hush while one of the men stepped out in the middle of the dance floor and spoke a brief welcome to Earl and me, and then he presented each of us with a box wrapped in tissue paper and tied with gay ribbon. Mine contained a lovely carving set and Earl's a gasoline lantern. Someone shouted, "Speech, speech!" and before I could stop them, they pushed me out on the dance floor with the announcer. I was so choked with emotion and so embarrassed at displaying my feelings that all I could say was "Thank you." Earl, quite undisturbed, thanked them at greater length—for the dance, for the presents, and for the neighborly thought which prompted the giving.

I supposed that the affair would be over after we had eaten, but, once refreshed, everyone danced with even greater zeal than before, and many were still going strong when we left at three-thirty.

All the way home I kept telling myself what a good time we had had. True, the evening had been pleasant, but there was something lacking. It wasn't anything that I could point to and say, "This is it." It was more like the small disturbance made when a stone is thrown into a pool of water, causing little ripples of doubt. I had expected the dance to be the mortar cementing me to the community life of my new home, but things hadn't worked out that way at all. Instead, I felt even further removed from my neighbors than I had when our only contact was the telephone. Because it had always been easy for me to make friends, it was hard to accept their standoffishness. I was bewildered, and my pride had suffered. The more I thought about it, the more angry I became.

When I complained to Earl, he said, "I think the trouble's with you, honey, always tryin' to figure out why people say this or do that. Instead of getting behind her with a prod pole and pushin', why don't you just let Nature take her course? There's nothing wrong with the situation that a little mindin' your own busi-

ness won't fix." His comment only made matters worse,
and I went to bed disgruntled with the world.

Next morning I was dead on my feet. Unaccustomed
to late hours, we overslept and everything got off to
a bad start. Even Virginia refused to co-operate, and
it took forever to get breakfast on the table. To aggra-
vate the situation, Jake said, "This coffee tastes like
dishwater."

"Well, I couldn't say, never having tasted dishwater,"
I snapped.

Earl was cross and out of sorts too, and he forgot to
kiss me good-by when he left for the woods, proof
enough to me in my black mood that he didn't love
me any more. An overcast sky didn't contribute anything to the tranquility of the family circle which,
that morning, might better have been described as a
"domestic corral." The cabin was dark at best, and on
that cheerless morning it was saturated with gloom.

While I sympathized with myself over the dishpan,
my predicament seemed to hinge on Earl and his com-
placent attitude. He was to blame for everything. Take
last night, for instance. It wouldn't have hurt him a
darned bit to step out of character and brag about me
a little to the neighbors. A little praise might have
lifted their opinion of me a lot. I finally gave up
trying to be reasonable and spent the rest of the gloomy
morning composing (to the accompaniment of distant
grumbling thunder) a long and caustic speech which
I planned to deliver the moment we were alone that
night.

Things went wrong with the crew, too, that day;
and Earl was so tired and so sleepy when he came in
from work that I didn't have nerve enough to say my
piece after all. Besides, my fury was relieved before

he got home, for that afternoon the ranger had left the mail; and it contained a check from my dad and an invitation to come home for a visit.

That evening, after the men had eaten and gone to their cabins, I handed the letter to Earl and watched him as he read it in silence, waiting expectantly for him to announce with emphasis, "No, you can't go. I can't get along without you." But instead he said, without any apparent feeling in his voice, "Maybe a visit home would be a nice change for you, honey. When do you plan to go?"

It took a moment to get my bearings. This was a pretty kettle of fish! I, who had intended to fire the first shot, was on the defensive again. Didn't he *care* if I left?

"Of course I can't go now and leave you with the boarders. I'll have to wait until they leave."

"You won't have to delay your trip on that account," Earl answered, throwing me even more off balance. "Now that the logs are all snaked in, I won't be needed in the woods any longer—so I'll have plenty of time to stir up the meals. Joe can take you into town when he goes for supplies at the end of the week."

This was even worse than I had anticipated. I was certainly important around here. Our honeymoon hadn't even lasted a year! Surely I deserved more consideration than this! Not only had he refused to forbid my leaving, but now it appeared he didn't even intend to put me safely on the train. Well, I certainly *would* go now. Wild horses couldn't stay me—and I'd take my time about coming back, too!

CHAPTER XV

Home to Mother

As the train sped across the plains of eastern Wyoming, carrying me farther and farther from the wilderness whose majesty had never failed to fascinate but whose isolation was driving me away, my thoughts kept turning backward over the past week, ending abruptly with a twinge of conscience when I recalled the injustice of my feeling toward Earl. Evidently he had intended all along to drive to town with Joe and me and put me on the train for Kansas; but since he had said nothing about his plans, I had taken it for granted that he would not accompany us. If he noticed the surprise in my eyes when, after dinner on Saturday, he had changed into his going-to-town clothes, he didn't show any sign of it. When Joe announced that he was ready to start, Earl picked up my suitcase and loaded it into the back of Joe's pickup and the three of us stepped into the cab.

The storm of the day before had spent itself, and the world was quilted with sunshine as we drove slowly down the rough road toward town on that May afternoon. Despite the battle raging inside me, I couldn't help enjoying the ride, the first in daylight since our frigid wedding trip the fall before.

The road followed the river, snaking its way down country through tunnels of lodgepole pine between the rugged rock formations of the Absaroka Mountains.

Two great presences, the restless river and the patient mountains, held the valley in their grip.

We, who lived along its shores or tributaries, loved the river, which played an important role in our isolated lives. From its creeks came all the water we used and drank; and good water it was, delicious to the taste and soft to the touch. During fishing season it furnished several varieties of trout for our table; and in the winter we cut ice from it, storing it in our private icehouses against the summer's need. Mink and otter, trapped along its shores, added to the winter's fur catch, and much of the driftwood washed up during high water was used in the fireplace through the long, hard winters.

In summer the dudes loved the sensation of fording the river on horseback, and a swim in its chilling waters was sheer adventure. We dug ditches leading from it to water our vegetable gardens, while farther down country it was used to irrigate huge tracts of farm land and to furnish power for lights and other electrical projects. It was a very busy river, minding its own business from sun to sun, but, fortunately for us, part of its business was to be beautiful. The man who wrote "A river is water in its loveliest form" must have been thinking of the Shoshone. Yes, the river was one of the friends I would miss most.

While the river attracted sportsmen with its good fishing and swimming, the mountains lured them with game and scenery, and there were many and varied trails leading into their expanses. Our wild meat pastured and fattened in the mountains and most of the fur-bearing animals we trapped made their homes there. We built our houses with the pine and fir which blanketed the gentler slopes, and the dead timber kept our home fires burning.

The Absarokas, with their jutting rocks and pinnacles, their network of creeks, their overlay of ridges, like backdrops in the theater, were friendly mountains. "More so than many of the folks who live in them," I thought, recalling the square dance.

They never thumbed their noses at us or gave us complexes, as the more lofty mountains do. Sometimes they were almost voluble, flashing their code of lights and shadows across the glens and meadows. Constancy was not one of their virtues, however, for we never looked up twice to the same view. Shifting clouds cast ever-changing shadows, and what was today a ridge standing out in bold relief was tomorrow a retiring coulee.

As we advanced farther down the valley, it widened to make room for several ranches of varying sizes. Earl helped me identify them with the owners who attended the dance.

The closer we got to town the less enthusiastic I became over the prospect of the journey, and had Earl so much as intimated that he didn't want me to go, I would have turned around and driven back to the ranch. I thought, "Summer is almost here, and there are too many things to do, too many places to explore, to ever get lonely or irritated in summer."

But no word of protest was spoken and the only indication that he wanted me to stay was shown in his lingering embrace beside the waiting train. Although

Denver is like no other place in the world

he didn't say so, I had a fleeting notion that he was afraid to let me go for fear I might never come back; and I couldn't think fast enough to invent an excuse for changing my mind at this eleventh hour.

As the train puffed its way into the mile-high Western city, I began to feel the thrill of excitement which Denver holds for every traveler. It is like no other place in the world—a city where a black derby and a cowboy sombrero can meet crown to crown without creating a feeling of out-of-placeness for either wearer; where miners and politicians, lumberjacks and college professors, mingle uncatalogued; where vacationers leave echoes of merriment behind them, breeding a carefree consciousness which one cannot feel in any other spot on earth.

Before we reached the station I could feel its urban atmosphere creeping into my backwoods bones, and I started making plans for the long layover between trains. First I would go window-shopping and maybe buy a new dress, and there would still be time left for a movie, a treat not enjoyed for months. Oh, it was going to be fun.

As a child with my parents, and later alone as a young woman, I had spent a lot of time in crowded cities, and I thrilled to the tempo of a bustling railroad station and a busy city street; but I hadn't remembered it as being anything like this. The traffic made my head swim. Thickets of people were scurrying hither and yon like ants uncovered by the removal of a stone. For a fleeting moment my eyes framed the picture of Earl and me as we snowshoed along the still white trail up Mesa Creek, the vast expanse of fresh snow unblemished by so much as the track of a field

mouse. Had I glimpsed paradise without even knowing it?

Suddenly the prospect of milling around all day in
that crowd seemed intolerable. After a leisurely lunch
at the station, I found a comfortable chair in the
ladies' lounge, where, having tired of watching the
people, I dug a book from my bag and sat quietly reading *The Lone Winter,* in complete accord with the
postman who took a walk on his holiday.

If someone had come up and asked me what the
book was about, I probably would have answered, "It's
a tale about a girl from Kansas who spent the winter
herding Shetland ponies in the mountains of Wyoming,"
for between every line of script I was inserting a line
of reminiscence, transplanting the story many miles
westward from its New England origin.

At last I gave up reading altogether and sat there
dreaming the hours away.

What better place to choose, I thought, than Denver
to take time out for a little constructive reasoning—
Denver, the halfway mark between the two forces
that were shaping my destiny.

There was no point in kidding myself any longer.
A fine roughneck I had turned out to be, taking the
first out by running home to Mother! Thank goodness, impulsiveness hadn't closed the door behind completely. True, I was on my way back to Kansas, but
only for a visit. I wondered how Earl was getting
along. I couldn't picture him as lonely, but surely he
must be missing me a little by now! But even if I
had been wrong, it didn't help any to blame myself
this way. Since I'd come this far, I might as well make
up my mind to enjoy the visit—and then hurry home
to Earl.

CHAPTER XVI

Mother Nature Holds the Reins

NEXT MORNING I was too excited to eat any breakfast
and peered avidly from the window at the country-
side, picking out landmarks along the way and linking
them with girlhood experiences. As we drew nearer
the old home town, I kept watching for the bluffs
where we used to picnic and which seemed so high
when I lived there. Then, as the train wheeled into
the city limits, I realized that I had missed them entirely. Because my eyes were gauged to the Rocky
Mountains, the bluffs had flattened out as easily as that.

The first rapture of reunion over, I found life
settling comfortably into well-remembered grooves.
Everything was right again, and living in a small Mid-
western town seemed a very desirable thing. It was
almost as quiet and peaceful as the country here, besides having the many mechanical conveniences that
made for easy living. Yes, a small town had everything,
everything except challenge, and I wasn't wanting any
more of that, thank you!

We had so much to talk about that long after the
brunch was consumed, we sat there visiting.

"Remember the time you stopped the polo game?" Mother asked.

"Remember? Can I ever forget it?" I recalled, as though it were yesterday, the nightmare of that experience.

The occasion was the championship game, and my chum and I had ridden our polo ponies over to the fort to watch it. As we approached, the game was in progress. A near-by steam roller suddenly let out a terrific snort; and my horse, startled, pricked up his ears and lunged toward the playing field—I pulled and jerked, entreated and commanded, but there was no holding him. A moment later I found myself surrounded by pounding hoofs and flying mallets. Above the din I heard an officer shout, "Get the hell out of here, you crazy kid!"

Of course they had to stop the game, shut off the steam roller, and get me safely out of the line of play before proceeding with the contest. For weeks I couldn't pass a soldier on the street without sensing an accusing finger and hearing a whispered accusation, "There goes the little squirt who stopped the polo game."

But work could not be put off indefinitely, so at last our round table of remembering broke up; and Dad went to the office and Mother to the kitchen, leaving me to unpack and get settled in my old room.

"Oh, Mother," I called, "everything is just as I left it."

"Why, of course. Did you expect to find it changed? It will always be your room, dear, waiting for you whenever you come back."

Come to think of it, I hadn't been gone a year. Why should I find things changed? I guess because life since leaving home had been so strange and new, I expected everything else to be different.

Then the phone started ringing. When would I be home to visitors? Could I come to Mary's for supper soon? How about a drive to the fort on Sunday? It seemed wonderful to be important again and I loved it. Life, for the next few days, was a whirlwind of activity and I scarcely had time to think of Earl.

And then the mail caught up with me. Earl's letter wasn't a long one and, except for the beginning and the end, endearing words were lacking; but his simple chronicle of the day's events, unembroidered with personal opinion, was so much like his talk that I felt I couldn't bear being separated a minute longer. I'd simply have to sprout a pair of wings and fly back to Wyoming.

"You missed a treat," he wrote. "I have been hunting horses all day, and dinnertime found me near Old Tex's so I stopped in for a handout. He had gathered a mess of potherbs and cooked them with potatoes and a ham hock. They were sure good eating."

Even reading about it made my mouth water, for ever since the first green sprout had stuck its curious nose through the warm earth along the margin of the trail behind our cabin, I had been eagerly awaiting this treat.

"The Indians cooked the first edible greens in pots over their campfires, and that's why the dish is called potherbs," Earl had explained. In our Wyoming region these greens included mustard, marsh marigold, lamb's-quarters, and cow parsnip.

I read and reread the letter, hoping to find some disguised message, but there was nothing there that could possibly be interpreted as a summons. I might have known that this was only wishful thinking, for he would never be the one to make the advances. I remembered the time last winter when I had waited alone in the forest. I'd felt abandoned then, but not forsaken like this. Guilt made the difference. Loneliness was bad medicine, but guilt was poison!

Earl's second letter came before a big dinner party. I was too busy getting ready for it to feel very homesick. When Anne issued the invitation she advised, "It isn't formal. Just wear your best short dinner dress."

My best short dinner dress—that was a laugh. I owned only one and, compared to hers, it was as up to date as last week's custard pie. I thanked her for the suggestion, though. "It's always nice to know. I might have come in overalls."

An attempt to erase the ravages of a rugged winter in one short afternoon was sheer agony. It had been ages since I took any interest in my face other than feeding it. The egg facial that stared at me from the mirror provoked a fit of giggles.

"If Earl could only see me now," I snickered, knowing that he probably wouldn't have said much of anything except, perhaps, to remark that he preferred his eggs fried, sunny side up.

Twelve guests sat down to Anne and Bob's beautiful table that evening. After we had eaten, Anne took me for a tour of the new house, and I admired the many convenient features. She confided that it was much more pretentious than they could afford.

"But then, we simply have to put up a good front if Bob expects to get ahead with his law practice."

Back in the living room, I relaxed in a down-filled chair as comfortable as a potted geranium, anticipating a cozy evening chatting about old times. We were scarcely seated before the conversation drifted into business and Bob, with exuberance, trailed off into a detailed description of his last law case, of the competition he had to buck in order to land it, and of the political wires pulled to bring it to a successful conclusion. Since our former visiting had consisted of reminiscing, I hadn't noticed before how remote the conversation was from anything that interested me. It was almost as if we were speaking different languages. All at once a yearning to be back in the hills gripped me. I longed to get as far away as possible from all this, to get back home where folks didn't put on airs or try to make impressions.

I was discovering, not without alarm, that, after less than a year in the wilderness, my interest in the outside was waning. Though many miles away, my world was still bounded on the west by Yellowstone Park, on the south by the Cougar Creek trap line, on the east by the party telephone wires, and on the north by the mysterious Continental Divide.

We had talked all through dinner and well into the evening, yet, so far, no one had so much as mentioned a horse, a trail, a wild animal, or a tree. I hadn't been aware before how important these things had become.

As my interest in the discussion lessened, the memory of our last dinner party—only we didn't call it that— at Gunbarrel grew clearer. Details, unnoticed at the time, stood out in relief against the unfamiliar background of Anne's living room. I recalled how, after the dishes were washed and put away, Ma Crouch had lighted the big kerosene lamp that hung from the center of the living room, and, having seated her guests in a half circle around the hearth, had drawn up her favorite rocking chair, the one without arms, to knit

Bob trailed off into a detailed description of his last law case

herself back to composure before the crackling fire. An air of contentment and fellowship permeated the room.

On that evening, instead of listening to sophisticated voices engaged in idle chatter, we had hearkened uneasily to the storm raging outside, each of us at intervals walking over to the window and peering through the thick white curtain of lashing snow as it pelted against the windowpanes. We were walled in so completely that we couldn't even see the creek which lay in frozen silence not twenty feet from the cabin. Steep canyon walls protected us from the full force of the wind, but we could hear it as it whistled through the tall pines above us, and we were grateful for the shelter of the strong log house and the friendliness of the open fire.

On nights like that there was even more to the fire than the warmth it gave out. I liked to think that the voices of the fire were really the murmur of summer winds rustling through the trees, and the songs of birds that perched on their branches. Some understanding woods magician may have stored them in the saps of the fire logs, to be released on cold, wintry evenings for the comfort and enjoyment of snowed-in folks like us.

The fire flickered and I tried to imagine feeling that way about a fireplace with a gas-burning log, like this one of Anne's; but I couldn't.

I remembered how, during the past winter, I had learned to love those days of complete tranquility, my heart softly beating to the hum of a secret content. It had been a new sensation to one whose days had always thrilled to the fullness of action, whose pattern of life had been a merry-go-round of comings and go-

ings. I who danced in the sun, had discovered a new
and satisfying contentment in slipping quietly into the
shadows against a patch of earth soft with snow and
pine needles. Oh, to be back there again, back in the
hills where I belonged.

Apparently nobody missed my animated repartee for
I was startled out of my reverie only when somebody
suggested a game of bridge. Having played nothing
but solo for almost a year, we might have been playing Old Maid for all the science I displayed, so when
someone said that it was time to go home, I was almost
rude in my eagerness to leave.

That night I lay awake trying to get things straight
in my mind. In a corner of the saddle shed stood an
old feedbox in which odd pieces of rope and strap
were stored. Someone had once added several balls of
binding twine, and every time we wanted a bit of
rope it was always tangled up with the loose ends of
the twine. Well, my mind was like that, a shambles of
loose ends. It didn't help a bit to remind myself that
this was the place in which I had been so content only
a few days ago. I was getting exactly what I wanted
—or had my reasoning become so snarled that, like the
Irishman, I didn't know what I wanted and wouldn't
be satisfied until I got it? When sleep finally came,
it was a troubled one, bringing dreams of Earl and
Wyoming, so I awoke to an issue as confused as ever.

Looking back over that following perplexing week,
I've often wondered how and when the problem would
have been solved had not Mother Nature stepped in
and supplied the same old solution.

Mother's suggestion to sleep late the morning after
the dinner party was heartily welcomed, so I was disappointed to awaken early, dizzy and nauseated.

"So much party fare," I thought, "has upset my homespun stomach."

I should have known better, for a cast-iron digestion had always been my boast. Only a few weeks before, when I was bragging about it, Earl had struck a ridiculous pose, and tottering on one boot heel, had quoted, "Food prepared for the stummick is what keeps alive the dude; but what saves my wife is a havin' a stummick prepared for the food."

When I didn't feel much better the next day, Mother took me to the family doctor, who diagnosed my symptoms without hesitation.

"Young lady, you haven't got anything catching. You've just started to raise a family and your whole system's upset. Mentally you'll be soaring in the clouds one minute and sinking in the mire the next. Just stop fretting and wait as patiently as you can."

I could remember feeling a little off-center several times during the past weeks but had attributed it to the spring thaw, the excitement of the trip, and Earl's attitude about my leaving. I should have know that something was amiss when a day in Denver created no elation. Funny, but it had never occurred to me that I might be pregnant. We had never talked much about a family, Earl and I, although we both liked children and hoped some day, in the dim future, to have some.

All I could think of for a few minutes was "What will Earl say?" Then, suddenly, I realized that here was a cause for rejoicing. This would be sufficient excuse for returning without losing face.

It was a whole evening's task, composing the letter to break the news to Earl. The first attempt, oozing maternity from every space and margin, was too drippy, so I tore it up and made a fresh start. Finally, after much rewriting, adding, omitting, and revising, the proper blend, I hoped, of dignity, humor, femininity and nonchalance was achieved, the result of which would set him to thinking.

The postman had scarcely picked up the mail next day before I started looking for an answer. A hazy recollection persists of having seen a lot of friends, done a lot of visiting, and lost a lot of meals during that long ten days of waiting, but the social activity only served as a background for the main issue of the day —watching for the mailman. Time consisted of a series of intervals between mail deliveries, and when at last the answer arrived I was so eager to open it that I tore a corner off and had to piece it together.

Earl didn't sound particularly excited about the prospect of becoming a father, and it was evident that in his eyes there was nothing phenomenal about my letter. Apparently he didn't consider having a baby any more unusual than taking a dose of sassafras tea to thin one's blood in spring, or changing to winter underwear after the first snowfall.

I could understand his attitude when, two years later, his mother came to visit us and told me about his birth.

"We were all out in the field, Dad and the children and me," she related, "when I began to feel the pains come. I didn't want to bother the men, being late with spring plowing, so I went in the house and had the baby all by myself. I couldn't go back to work in the field for about a week, but I did the cooking and housework like always."

Having sprung from such hardy stock, how could he be expected to get excited over having a baby, eight months hence?

But I wasn't too disappointed about his reaction, for

the words I wanted most to hear were there. Triumphantly I read them over and over—only seven little words but they were as eloquent as the Gettysburg Address, and as emancipating.

He had written at the end of the letter, "When will you be coming home, honey?"

CHAPTER XVII

Trail Blazing

THAT FIRST SUMMER of our marriage was the most carefree one of my life.

Because the bunkhouse was meant to house the cowboys, we had moved out before the arrival of the first dude; in fact, Earl had made the change while I was away and set up temporary residence in a tent down by the river. He laid a board floor and set up sidewalls of pine lumber to make it easier to clean.

Earl got up early and ate breakfast at the lodge. Since the dudes spent most of their day in the saddle, either riding between meals or taking all-day trips, I seldom saw him until suppertime. I could hardly wait until he got home so I could worm a recital of the day's activities from him. Did anybody fall off? How many new dudes? Any silly questions today? Judging from some of the questions, you'd think the ones who asked them had never even read a book. One man asked if they took the horses' shoes off every night. Riding through a grove of aspen trees, a lady wanted to know if that was where aspirin came from. Once on a pack trip Earl guided a party over the Continental Divide through Two Oceans Pass, where the water flows to both the Pacific and the Atlantic. One dudine exclaimed, "Oh, I'm sorry it's so cloudy. It would be such fun to see both oceans at the same time."

Frequently a newcomer had to be instructed on how to light a kerosene lamp. One of the guests brought hers to the office and asked, "How do you light this thing? I've thrown three matches down the chimney, and they just go out."

"Westerners never act that dumb when they go East," Earl complained. "If they'd keep their eyes open and their mouths shut, nobody would know how ignorant they are."

He came home one evening with his arms full of puppy, the softest, fluffiest, cutest little pup you ever saw.

"Somebody left it at the lodge. Don't you think it will be nice to have a puppy all housebroke before the baby comes?"

One look from the pleading puppy eyes and I signed adoption papers. He was golden-yellow with a white ring around his neck, so we called him Ring. Now I had a dog to go with my horse.

When Earl met the train in town on my way back from Kansas, we had gone to the doctor and I asked him about riding, expecting thumbs down on such strenuous exercise. I was surprised when he said, "I can't see as riding will do any harm as long as you stay away from bucking broncos—and there's room in the saddle for the two of you."

He told me something else, too, and for once I was glad Earl wasn't curious and had remained in the lobby during the interview. No need to tell him everything—besides, even doctors sometimes made mistakes.

A baby delivered by Caesarean section *sounded* serious

but I wasn't afraid. "If I tell Earl," I rationalized, "he'll insist on sending me to town before we get snowed in and that might spoil our Christmas! It isn't as if there's any real danger anyway." With that I dismissed it from my mind.

A collection of wild flowers started the previous summer in Yellowstone had developed into a driving hobby, so I was looking forward to days joyfully spent in the forest looking for new specimens.

Before permitting me to ride alone, Earl issued some instructions.

"Never leave home without a handful of matches in your pocket and a slicker tied behind your saddle," he said. "And if you lose your bearin's and haven't a horse to lead you home, follow a crick to the river and finally you'll come to a cabin. If it gets dark, build a fire and stay put till mornin'. If you get panicky, don't move. Stay where you are till the mood passes."

"I won't get lost," I replied confidently. "I'll just remember the landmarks and come back the same way I went."

"I bet you will! Just like you remember to stuff Virginia before she goes out!"

For once I didn't have an answer.

Ring and Badger and I had a wonderful summer following the beckoning trails up the canyons and over the meadows. Surely life can hold no pleasure comparable to that of riding through virgin forest, your only companions a dog and a horse!

Wild flowers were everywhere. Along the water's edge grew yellow monkey flower, marsh marigolds, and fringed gentians, while yellow arnica, red paintbrush, blue lupine, and dainty Queen Anne's lace designed a floral pattern along the carpet of pine needles under the trees. On the steep arid hillsides among the rocks, the same colors were repeated in stonecrop, scarlet bugler, harebells, and locoweed.

One morning we stumbled onto a wild strawberry patch. The sweet aroma carried on a gentle breeze directed us to it. Some of the underleaves on the lacy plants had already turned a delicate pink, so it was hard to see the berries at first. The best way to distinguish them from the foliage was to lie down in the patch and look up. Not having anything to carry them in, I ate my fill. Next time I would bring a pail. "How could so much sweetness be packed into such a tiny berry?" I wondered.

And so wild berry picking was added to my list of "must do's." The wild raspberries, currants, gooseberries and, later in the season, the chokecherries, elderberries, and Oregon grape, were familiar; but I had never seen a thimbleberry before. They grow on tall bushes with slender, swaying branches, the leaves resembling those of the raspberry, only larger. The fruit is like a raspberry, fitting over your little finger like a thimble.

As I picked, I recalled how much Earl liked the homemade jams and jellies Ma Crouch served and determined that next year we, too, would have "glasses of glory" to brighten the shelves in our root cellar.

Ma Crouch shared with me many of her experiments with wild fruit. From her I learned that Oregon grape juice made excellent jelly if diluted with equal parts of apple juice. One of her most mystifying jellies was made from rose berries. She picked the red seed pods from wild rose bushes, barely covered them with water, and stewed them slowly until they could be mashed

Surely life can hold no pleasure comparable to that of riding through virgin forest, your only companions a dog and a horse.

with a spoon, then strained the juice through cloth. To one cup of the juice she added two of apple juice and made a jelly that defied identity.

There were other berries, too, strange exotic ones which I was tempted to sample—then I'd remember the camass bulbs and refrain.

I'd heard that the Indians ate camass bulbs in times of famine. I wanted my baby to be rugged and "out-doorsy," and wasn't there an old wives' tale that said the things a pregnant woman did and ate influenced the character of the child? The bulbs were disappoint-ingly slimy and tasteless. I dug up one to take home to Earl as a joke, but instead of laughing about it, he scolded, "After this, be careful what you eat. There's two kinds of camass and the only way you can tell the difference is by the flower. Death camass has a white blossom, the other a blue. You're just lucky you ate the right one. If you don't watch your step, I'll hide your shoes and plant cactus 'round the door."

On flower-picking excursions I took a sack lunch and shared my sandwiches with Ring while Badger grazed contentedly on the meadow, his bit removed from his mouth. Lying there under the pines, I'd fol-low the pattern of needle and branch against the blue sky, watching it shift into different designs as the soft wind disturbed the trees. It was the nearest to heaven I'll ever be!

Ring loved to chase field mice and rabbits along the way, and Badger preferred meandering around with us to the monotony of traveling the same dusty dude trails day after day.

When I'd spot a specimen in an inaccessible spot, I'd dismount, drop my reins, and amble off, sometimes quite a distance; but Badger always stayed where I left him. Lucky for me that he was dependable, because I didn't have any more sense of direction than a feather.

The first time I disputed the right of way with him, we strayed for miles, until, tired of reining him, I gave him his head. He led us back to the forks of the trail, took the opposite turn, and soon we were back on the creek, down the river, and home.

My first all-day trip with the dudes was amusing. Three dudines fell off their horses; one fainted; and five had to be led across the river. One woman refused to drink from the creek—the ranch water was piped from one just like it—and complained about being thirsty all the way up Eagle Creek and back; and one of the men had an argument with his wife and refused to ride with her any longer.

Earl guided; and Don, another cowboy, brought up the rear with the pack horse. Between them rode a group of about twenty-five swamp angels, a few regulars, and me.

The guest list at the ranch was made up of three distinct types of dudes: the "regulars," guests who came to the ranch to see the scenery and enjoy ranch life, the majority of whom were easy to handle, pleasant to know, and nice to remember; the "wild bunch," made up largely of youngsters between the ages of ten and eighteen, who, if unrestrained, would ride the hides off the horses; and the "swamp angels," consisting of the nervous, high-strung type, mostly women.

"What on earth is a 'swamp angel'?" I inquired, the first time I heard Earl use the term.

"A 'swamp angel' is a dudine with her brains knocked out. I say 'her' because most of them are female. A

male swamp angel is about the lowest form of plant
life.

"A genuine swamp angel," he continued, "squeals
every time her horse steps over a bump on the trail;
she keeps the guide busy lengthening and shortening
her stirrup straps, hangs onto the saddle horn with
both hands whenever the trail leads over a rise, and
has to be led across all the steep and frightening places.
Strangely enough, she's deadly afraid of water but
wouldn't miss fording the river because it will make
'such a good letter home.' "

Many of them appeared at the corral decked out in
the most ungodly riding outfits, and most of them
had never been on a horse before. Unfortunately, they
too often outnumbered the other guests two to one.

The guide assigned to wrangle a group like this
needed a lot of patience, for there is nothing more
aggravating than a bunch of ruffled swamp angels.

The wild bunch was another problem.

"They've got a notion," Earl said, "that a vacation
on a dude ranch is their chance to live through a
Western thriller. If you'd let 'em, they'd gallop off
in high, break all the rules, and pay no attention to
the guide. I never take 'em on the highway or up a
woods road to ride."

"I should think they'd be perfectly safe on a woods
road," I put in.

"Nope," he countered, "the narrower the trail the
better. Dude horses are trained to travel single file;
and on a narrow trail, a guide can keep the wild bunch
behind him. If a feller gave those kids their head
there'd be lame horses and crippled dudes strung all
over the mountains. Funny thing, though, the girls
are a lot better behaved than the boys."

Our destination that day was Eagle Creek Meadows. The trail up the creek was full of surprises. One minute we'd be riding serenely through forest, then turn with a bend in the trail to glimpse jagged mountain peaks in the near distance, some of them still capped with snow. As the trail climbed higher, miniature streams grew more abundant, the water churning into cascades as it tumbled down the mountainsides. Sometimes the stream would stop to rest in a small pool beside a shady glen, where the delightful grace of ferns mingled with the delicate undergrowth of the forest. Here we would all dismount and drink. Water from one of these pools was as exhilarating as a draft of mellow wine.

It was almost noon when we reached the picnic ground. Eagle Creek Meadows were like a tapestry, embroidered with masses of vividly colored wild flowers. We had to hopscotch to keep from crushing the lovely blossoms. In their blue intensity, the Alpine forget-me-nots vied with the Wyoming sky. From a distance the clumps of deer moss that dotted the meadow looked like whitewashed stones. Rosy wild geraniums, yellow cinquefoil, red paintbrush, purple elephant-heads, and deep pink wild roses added to the color harmony.

Earl and Don removed the provisions from the pack horse and cooked the dinner over a campfire on a grassy plot near the creek. Remembering that meal is refreshment in itself. We had bacon and eggs, baked beans, cowboy spuds, coffee, and raisin cake.

To prepare cowboy spuds, Earl pared and sliced enough for the group, adding sliced onions and salt and pepper to taste. Then he put them in a stew pan and barely covered them with water, cooked them slowly until tender, added a generous hunk of butter, and they were ready for the hungry riders. Almost everyone took a second helping, and from then on they were a favorite dish in our family.

In the party were a young doctor and his wife. He was a prince of a fellow, but she was a typical swamp angel. On the way home she was the first to be led across the river. She shut her eyes and held fast to the saddle horn with both hands. When her horse slipped on a rock or stepped into a hole in the river bed, she'd shriek and frighten all the other horses.

As Earl handed her the reins, he warned, "Hold back your horse or he'll head for the barn!" Instead, she dropped the reins, kicked her horse in the flanks, and fell to the ground in a dead faint.

Watching her, my heart missed a beat. She lay so still I thought she was dead. I looked fearfully at her husband, but he wasn't even disturbed.

"She'll come out of it," he said as he spurred his horse into the river. "She faints easily."

He was right. She came to after a little shaking, no worse for her tumble.

Earl said, "It's over a mile to the corral. You can ride in my saddle and I'll ride double behind."

As Earl helped her mount, Buddy, his horse, threw his head and hit her square in the eye.

By the time she got back to the ranch her eye had swollen into a real shiner; and she spent the rest of the week in her cabin. Her vacation had turned out to be a flop in more ways than one.

I identified sixty-two wild flowers on that trip. While many of them were not in my collection, I didn't bring home a single new specimen! You couldn't stop a procession of twenty-eight riders just to pick a wild flower.

After that I voted for the solitary trips. It was more fun to stop when and where I wanted to, and how I hated to pass up a new specimen!

CHAPTER XVIII

Exercise the Critter

"YOU'LL FIND your new life interesting," Ma Crouch said in one of our mail-day conversations. "A dude wrangler's wife leads two lives. In summer your interest will center around the dudes and roughnecks at the lodge, while in winter your neighbors will occupy the limelight."

It was true. We seldom saw our neighbors during the summer for they were as busy as we. Lucky for me, that summer didn't last long enough for my ego to soar to unknown heights, for I was considered a native by the dudes and looked upon with envy. To be turned loose in the mountains with a horse and a dog was, to them, a passport to paradise. Anyone so privileged must be a real pioneer!

At the first sign of smugness I'd saddle my horse and take off for a visit with Old Tex, who knew just how to whittle me down to my own size. While he was always friendly, I imagined that he thought mine a useless kind of life.

"Women nowadays," he said, "don't keep busy enough to keep out o' trouble. Take my Aunt Nell, fer instance. There wuz a woman! She wuzzent much of a horsback rider; but she wuz a good hand with a team an' drove her fam'ly of nine young'uns clean from Ioway to the Panhandle, while Uncle Ned rode on ahead horseback to pick out campin' sites. Besides doin' her own housekeepin', which women jest natural-ly took for granted them days, she made cheese an' soap, rendered out the lard an' cured the ham an' bacons whenever Uncle Ned butchered a hog. He give her the bum lambs to raise an' she carded, spun, an' wove the wool into cloth, an' then of an evenin' when she wuz restin' she'd sew it into clothes for the family.

"Of an afternoon she liked to wander off into the woods an' gather wild berries fer jelly, an' roots fer makin' dye to color the rags she braided into rugs. In her spare time she knitted socks an' caps and mittens fer the kids an' pieced quilts an' tied comforters. She even dipped the candles they used fer lights. What this world needs nowadays is more women like Aunt Nell."

I couldn't tell whether he was poking fun at me, or really thought I ought to be doing some of the things Aunt Nell did, instead of gadding around on a horse.

That's what made it so exasperating—I was never able to determine the relationship between us. I was so desirous of his approval and so conscious of my limitations that I built up false interpretations of every-thing he said.

Although he lived in a one-room log cabin and had never owned an automobile—"a feller with two good laigs don't need four wheels," he contended—Old Tex was rich. He had what he wanted and lived the life he liked; he feared nothing; he envied no one; he never looked up or down at a living soul. He got more satisfaction from helping others develop their talents than he did from flaunting his own wisdom.

While Earl could do anything that had to be done around a ranch, he was a poor teacher, so I had Tex to thank for many of the things I learned. He was always engaged in some interesting project and was very nearly self-sufficient, even making his own gloves from the hides of animals he killed and tanned himself.

"Every animal is supposed to have enough brains in his head to tan his own hide," he told me as he explained the process.

"Out on the range whenever we found a bleached skull, we could allus tell if it was Injun killed by the hole in the head where the brains wuz took out. That's where I learned to make leather—from the Injuns."

"It looks like soapsuds," I said, peering into the tub where the hides were soaking.

"Yup," he replied, "but it's only brains beat up to a froth in water. Depends on the size and thickness of the hide how long it has to soak. Sometimes it takes a week or more."

"How can you tell when it has soaked long enough?" I inquired.

"When you look at it edgewise an' it's porous and you don't see no raw streak between the two sides, it's done an' can be hung on a line to drip dry. When most of the water's evaporated but the skin's still damp, it's time to pull an' work an' knead it till it's soft and pliable. That's when I wish I had me a squaw to chew the hide soft an' save me all that work."

I laughed and looked quizzically at Earl, who explained, "Tex isn't joking. Squaws without any teeth really do chew the hides until they are soft."

"Does the hair come off in the brain solution?" I asked.

"No," Tex answered, "I took that off first with wood ashes. Last week I put the hide in a wooden tub, hair side up, and sprinkled a bucketful of wood ashes over it an' then covered it with water an' left it to soak until the hair began to slip. Then I stretched the hide out tight on the floor an' nailed it down around the edges. Next I scraped it clean on both sides with this homemade scraper." He indicated a gadget made of an old file.

"When all of the hair on the outside and flesh on the inside is scraped off," he continued, "I put the hide in the brain solution an' go on with the tannin' like I told you."

On these visits we drank coffee, and he was sure to have sour-dough biscuits or cinnamon buns to eat with it. His cabin was neat and uncluttered and had an air of coziness. It made me think of rooms described in Western novels.

In a far corner stood a wood bunk bed. Instead of springs, strips of rawhide had been interwoven and tacked to the baseboards. Over several sugans—his word for quilts—a canvas bed tarp was spread and the bed used as a couch in the daytime. The first time I sat down on it, I exclaimed, "Tex, what on earth do you have in your bed? It rattles!"

"Oh," he replied, "that's jest straw. It's gittin' kinda brittle. Needs refillin'. I put fresh in every fall when the new crop's harvested. I jest can't git my rest a-layin' on one of those new-fangled mattresses."

The square kitchen table standing near the cookstove wasn't covered with oilcloth as most bachelor's tables were, but the boards were clean and sanitary.

They had a scrubbed-often look. Shed deer horns were nailed to the wall in several places; and on these hung an old hat, a pair of chaps, a gun in its holster, and other Western regalia. A calendar picturing a pretty girl in a bathing suit was the only ornament.

Household operating expenses must have been practically nil. Old Tex even opened cans with his pocketknife. His butcher knife was handmade from an old file and had a deer-horn handle. It was as sharp as a razor.

He used only one dishtowel at a time and boiled it after each using, adding a few chips of homemade lye soap to the water. No wonder it was so white. After the dishes were washed, he'd wipe out the grease from the inside of the dishpan with a piece of paper and rub it on the top of the cookstove. "Keeps it nice and shiny," he said proudly.

Hanging on the wall was an odd contraption made from a tin can.

"It's a bachelor's lantern," Tex replied in answer to my query.

"Oh, I'd love to have one like it. No smoky chimney to clean. Will you make one for me sometime?"

"Sure." He smiled. "Might as well do it now."

About midway on the rounded side of an open Number 10 tin can, he cut a cross three quarters of an inch long, punching the four points to the inside. From the outside, he poked a kitchen candle through the hole about three inches, leaving the rest sticking out. Then, on the side of the can opposite the candle, he punched two small holes, one near the rim and one near the bottom, and fastened a piece of wire from one to the other for a bail.

Paul Reeve Martin

"*Next I scraped it clean on both sides with this homemade scraper*"

For years we used lanterns made that way and found them very useful on camping trips.

It was Old Tex who taught me how to manipulate my end of a crosscut saw.

One day in early autumn I mentioned that several times I had wanted to help Earl with the sawing, but hadn't offered to for fear I'd be more of a hindrance than a help.

"Come on out to the woodpile," Tex suggested, "and I'll give you a lesson. Then you kin pretend to catch on fast the first time you offer to lend Earl a hand. Besides, the work will do you good."

At the woodpile, having rolled a log onto the saw-horse, he instructed, "Now, sawin' wood is jest like swimmin'. If you make hard work of it, you git into trouble. Jest take it easy-like an' let the weight an' the sharp-edged teeth do the work. You jest do the guidin'."

I took a firm grip on the saw handle and, with a nervous hand, concentrated as hard as possible; but we had only sawed back and forth a few times before the saw started to bind. I stopped and looked up at Old Tex.

"Now what have I done?"

"Nothin' that a little teamwork can't fix," he answered, "but mebbe we'd better set an' rest a spell before we try again. You worked so hard you're plumb out o' breath."

"That's not the only reason," I confessed. "Tex, did you know that I am going to have a baby?"

"Of course I did," he answered with a smile. "Why else did you think I was givin' you all this exercise? Out on the range we figger when a critter is goin' to calve we'd better get her out in the field where she

can run around a little an' limber up, thet it would
be easier on her when her time come. Works the same
with humans. When I wuz a kid, women didn't think
no more about hevin' a young'un than goin' to bed
at night or gettin' up in the mornin'. They wuz tough,
thet's why. They didn't have hospitals to lay around
in an' soften up. When do you figger on havin' him?"

"I think about the first of January," I replied. "I'm
not sure."

"Well, don't worry none, an' you'll git along all
right. Lots of women afore your time have raised
kids in these mountains, an' they've turned out jest
as healthy as the town-bred ones, mebbe healthier."

When we rose to resume our sawing, he warned,
"This time don't push none at all an' only pull a little
mite. It don't take strength to run a crosscut saw.
Once you get it in your head it's easy, it almost does
itself."

So I relaxed and was surprised at how easily the
saw moved back and forth. A few moments later,
we heard the musical thud of the end as it fell to the
ground, followed by another and another; and soon
we had finished the log.

"That was a right good job," Old Tex surprised me
by saying. "You done a lot better'n a couple of dude
boys from the lodge who come down one afternoon
an' offered to saw up some wood. They sure dulled
my saw fer me; an' if I'da had my old teeth back, I
could a beavered it down faster'n they did."

I blushed with pleasure, but wasn't nearly as excited
as I supposed I would be.

"A month ago," I thought, "a compliment from
Old Tex would have set my head in a whirl."

Could this be a good sign?

CHAPTER XIX

Open House

STANDING IN Ma Crouch's kitchen looking out upon another autumn, I had to pinch myself to prove I wasn't dreaming. Could it be possible that the red and yellow ribbon winding its way to the river marked Gunbarrel Creek? Could the colorful tapestry spread out before me really be *my own* back yard?

The buildings were strung along the creek much as they were at Timber Lodge, but Gunbarrel ran down a narrow canyon—that's how it got its name—and there was only room on one side for the cabins. There were three single ones in front of the main house, and behind, where the canyon widened, three double ones stood with their backs against the mountain. Nearer the creek were the bathhouse, garage, and icehouse. Just above the icehouse the creek turned to the east, hugging the bank on our side, but leaving enough flat space on the other to accommodate the corrals and barn.

On this ravishing fall day the beauty of the landscape almost took your breath away. The mountain maples were flinging wild flames to the wind, their leaf embers floating lazily to the ground where they added a splash of red to the yellow of the aspen leaves which covered it.

"Oh," I exclaimed in ecstasy, "what have I done to deserve all this?"

It had all come about so unexpectedly. One evening, while we were still living at Timber Lodge, Earl confided, "Due to Ma's health, the Crouches have decided to sell out and move to Oregon. I wish we had the capital to swing the deal. It would be a swell setup for us."

Then had followed a stream of letters to and from Kansas until, the first thing we knew, we were in possession of a small dude ranch and could look forward to a more comfortable winter. No doubt Dad was influenced by the prospect of a grandchild. We reveled in all the extra room.

And now the lady of the house standing beside the kitchen stove was none other than I. I imagined that I could see the new Virginia blink disapprovingly, as though she couldn't quite bring herself to accept the slovenly ways of the new cook, but, still, she had decided to suspend judgment until I had shown my incompetence.

There was no getting around it; the house was already acquiring that cluttered look. In spite of repeated resolutions to be neat, my house always got that way. Perhaps it's because I'm the adhesive type; dirt sticks to me at the slightest contact. To complicate matters, Earl and I both prefer homemade rugs on our floor, hides and hunting trophies on our walls, rough draperies at the windows, and sofa pillows scattered over a wool-covered couch, all dust catchers. The only thing to be said in my favor is that I manage to keep my dirt fresh.

When we first moved, I tried my best to be immaculate; and the air was punctuated with warnings. "Don't forget to wipe your feet when you come in!" "Watch out for your ashes!" "Please put the catalogs back where you found them."

Earl finally complained.

"I hope you get over this neat spell before next dude season. I don't mind a little clutter; fact is, I prefer it to being nagged at, and it's the same with the dudes. That's one of the best things about a ranch vacation—freedom from all the fuss about dirt and disorder. I wouldn't try so hard to improve your housekeeping if I were you. I like you best as you are naturally."

Already tired of the new order, I was only too glad to take his advice. Later a neighbor, noted for her lack of diplomacy, remarked, "I wish I could be a careless housekeeper like you. I'd have more time to read and knit and enjoy my family."

Earl, who seldom gave tongue to a bald-faced compliment, surprised me by his bristled retort.

"Careless housekeeper? You mean 'comfortable,' don't you?"

How I ever mustered enough courage to try to fill Ma Crouch's shoes I'll never know. Dispensing hospitality was no problem, for I liked all kinds of people. It was the cooking that floored me. No one with a full stomach ever knocked at our door.

Apparently Earl knew everybody in the country, and having spent considerable time riding the grub line himself, he was glad for the chance to return past favors. He had been raised in a day when a ranch visitor was greeted with the invitation, "Come in and stay a week and, if you like it, make us a visit."

There were times when he carried this make-yourself-at-home business a little too far. I recall one evening when two strangers rode in on horseback at suppertime. Earl helped them care for their horses and invited them to eat. I was just setting the table as they passed through the kitchen, and he turned to me and asked, "Honey, will you put on a couple extra plates for these fellows?"

When he didn't introduce them, I made a mental note to remind him that night not to get careless about his manners, even though we did live in the sticks.

The men were typical of our country, closemouthed and courteous. As they visited around the fire after supper, their conversation was without locale. They talked easily of hunting and horses while I sat listening, consumed with curiosity. Nobody asked any questions or mentioned any names. That night, after we retired, I asked Earl who they were and where they were going.

"I haven't the slightest idea."

"Don't you intend to find out before they leave in the morning?" I insisted. "Who knows, they might even be wanted by the law."

"If they are, it's none of our business," was his answer. "If they want us to know who they are, they'll tell us."

Next morning they offered to pay for their visit; but since it was out of season, Earl refused to take anything, inviting them instead to drop in anytime they happened over our way. We never saw them again, and I'm still wondering who they were and where they were going.

A complete absence of curiosity was an inherent trait of the men in the community. It never occurred to Earl to be curious about anything that didn't concern him. To him a free exchange of thoughts and ideas was not one of the requirements for a good marriage. His thoughts were his own as my thoughts were mine, and any curiosity regarding them was being just plain nosy.

One day that fall we were so late getting home after a business trip that we popped into bed without even building a fire. In the middle of the night, I felt something lumpy under my head and reached to find the cap I had worn to town bunched up on my pillow.

Next morning I said to Earl, "Didn't you notice that I wore my cap to bed last night?"

"Yes, I did," he answered.

"Then why on earth didn't you tell me?"

"Well, I figured if you wanted to wear your cap to bed it was your affair," he replied.

"I wonder if you'd consider it any of your business if I stepped out in the nude sometime?" was my sarcastic retort.

Hospitality? I had it rammed down my throat in large doses all that fall, and even into the dead of winter we had frequent company. When they couldn't come by car, they came on horseback; and when they couldn't ride a horse through the snowdrifts, they came on snowshoes or skis. And always they came hungry. In winter most of our company consisted of trappers who, tiring of their own food and company, made regular trips down to the ranch. I generally enjoyed their visits as much as Earl; but as my waiting time grew shorter and my girth larger, there were days when I was far too uncomfortable to welcome company. One washday stands out in particular.

It was late in the hunting season. We had eaten a

And always they came hungry

sketchy lunch at noon, and the dirty dishes still stood in the wooden sink. It was after two when I glanced through the window and saw Earl and two strangers walk up to the hitching rack and tie their horses. I stretched my aching back and dried my hands on a towel in order to acknowledge their introduction, after which Earl asked, "Can you fix these fellows up a bite of lunch? They haven't eaten since breakfast and must be pretty hungry."

It was one of those days when there wasn't a thing left over, and I had to start from scratch! Earl whittled some steaks from a hind quarter of deer, and I opened a can of corn and fried some potatoes. I kept a calm exterior, although inside my temperature was boiling. Even the fact that one of the men was Buffalo Bill's grandson didn't make it any easier.

When they were fed and on their way, I scrubbed even more vigorously, rehearsing over the washtub several cutting remarks I planned to unleash the minute Earl returned. It was some time before he got back, however, so I had boiled down to a simmer and only inquired coolly, "Earl, where did you pick up those men?"

"Oh," he replied, "I was riding through the Palisades and met them goin' down the river as I came up. I asked them when they ate last and they said not since breakfast, so I invited them to ride back to the house for a bite. You didn't mind, did you?"

"Mind?" I exploded. "I don't mind your asking people to eat at mealtime when they come by the house, but this thing of going *down* the river and dragging a couple of fellow *back* two miles for a special meal on washday is carrying hospitality a little too far."

When Earl walked over to the sink and began quietly to wash up the dishes, I really felt ashamed.

Now that I had a home of my own, I was determined to keep up the amenities and, in the matter of table-cloths and napkins, I would consider no compromise —oilcloth was not for us!" The napkins were the first to go. Religiously I put them on and took them off, but always only one was used. When I mentioned it to Earl, he said he hadn't spilled his food since his mother took him out of bibs. Eventually I gave up putting them on, but I still clung tenaciously to the tablecloths. Having to wash them on the board when water was scarce put an end to them, and the table-cloths were relegated to company along with the nap-kins. We were eating off oilcloth—and liking it.

Like the bears, we started burrowing in soon after the first snowstorm. Our first move took us from the combined office-bedroom behind the house into the front bedroom of the main house, occupied in summer by dudes who preferred a reasonable facsimile of hotel accommodations to private cabins. Here we slept com-fortably in twin beds until the mercury took another drop and I had to wear a wool sweater and wool socks to bed. Then we moved into the double bed in the back bedroom and changed from sheets to flannel blan-kets, adding an eider-down sleeping bag to our covers and taking a hot-water bottle to bed with us.

One morning, when I awoke to find the hot-water bottle wedged between the mattress and the foot of the bed, frozen solid, Earl announced, "Well, I guess that means it's time to move south for the winter."

This time we literally picked up our bed and walked —into the living room where we set it up beside the open fireplace. There, in our combination living room, bedroom, dog kennel, and bath, we slept for the rest of the winter.

It was fun lying there in the dark, watching the tongues of flame from the open fire as they flickered softly on the walls and ceiling, the darkness deepening as the flames died into embers.

I got a lot of practice building fires, for Dan Crouch wasn't near to call me up and tell me to put another stick of wood on the fire as he had the winter before. Besides Virginia and the fireplace, there was also a quick-heating wood stove at the other end of the living room to tend; and one of them was always in the process of going out or being started.

Earl taught me how to build a fire in the fireplace. The first requisite was a good backlog, so the largest and greenest of the fire logs were set aside for that purpose. The fire was built in front of the backlog so the heat would radiate into the room instead of flowing up the chimney. Sometimes a backlog lasted all night or longer, but it was necessary to replenish the front ones often.

Earl still started his fires with prayer sticks; but I wasn't very handy with a knife so I used another method. In front of the backlog I set two sticks of split wood parallel to each other, the ends facing the hearth. On these were placed some crumpled paper and small wood, with the logs on top. The two bottom pieces provided the necessary draft.

Instead of judging a man's thrift by his bank account, we used his woodpile as a measuring stick. Most of the ranches had two, one in the back yard and the other on the front porch.

"This is a funny country," a dudine once remarked to Earl. "People always enter the back door when

they come to visit and pile their firewood on the front
porch."

The living room at Gunbarrel Lodge was filled with
friendly associations. You had only to step through
its door to feel warm arms around your shoulders, as
though a lot of sunshine and good cheer had been
absorbed by its house logs through years of gracious
living. I half expected them to sprout new branches
and burst out in fresh greenery, the room was that alive.

As I cleaned the room and made a place for the
bed and dresser, I kept recalling little conversations
Ma Crouch and I had had, until it almost seemed as
though she were there with me. I don't think her
spirit ever entirely left that room. Some intangible
bit of her was left behind in the cabin and was as
enduring as the house logs and the homemade furniture.

Catalogs were as much a part of a ranch home as
any of its furnishings; and in ours, "Monkey Ward"
and "Rears Sawbuck," as we affectionately dubbed
them, were in constant use. The current numbers were
dog-eared before their successors arrived. One of my
favorite winter pastimes was making out an order of
household goods, furnishing whole rooms from wall-
paper to rugs. Of course the orders were never mailed.
Our real orders were for long underwear, woolen shirts
and socks, steel traps, knitting worsted, and other practical items. At that time the mail-order catalogs didn't
concentrate as much on fashion as they do now. Most
of the clothing was, as Earl put it, "Not much for
style but hell for stout."

Shopping by catalog was much more exciting than
buying things in stores, for there was always the thrill
of getting a package in the mail.

Although the old house was never unfriendly, there

were times when I felt like an intruder, for I knew how much it must miss its former occupants. I could just see Ma Crouch taking a last lingering look at her old home as she said in farewell, "Good-by, old house, be good to your new mistress. Although her ways may seem strange, bear with her; and in time you'll learn to love her the same as you do me."

That was why I didn't rearrange the furniture any more than necessary, why I left her knitting chair standing by the fireplace and often knitted in it myself. I imagined that the cabin felt more comfortable that way.

"Dear me," I mused, "why don't I, now that I'm beginning to earn Old Tex's respect, let well enough alone and not create another obstacle in the person of an old log house?"

CHAPTER XX

Wilderness Pleasures

ASIDE FROM more responsibility and room, living conditions weren't very different at Gunbarrel from those at Timber Lodge the year before.

Our plumbing froze up in the winter just as it had done at the bunkhouse; and hurrying feet wore a path from the kitchen door to our "Swiss Chalet" on the hillside, where out-of-date catalogs furnished the bulk of our reading material. But on such an icy seat there was no incentive to linger. A poem tacked on the wall expressed our sentiments precisely.

> We did our duties promptly;
> There one purpose swayed the mind.
> We tarried not, nor lingered long,
> With what we left behind.

The first time Earl heard me call our outside toilet the "Swiss Chalet," he said disgustedly, "I think that's silly, calling an outhouse by such a name."

To him anything except plain "Men" or "Women" was affectation, like "cantering down the pawth" instead of "loping down the trail."

During the past summer the Forest Service had improved the campgrounds, and the toilets now boasted a new form of architecture and looked like woodsheds. They also bore the more refined name of "Comfort Stations."

"Comfort Stations! Bah!" was Earl's reaction.

Weather still ruled our days. Its fiscal year began in the fall when we waved good-by to the last dude and Sylvan Pass was snowed in for the winter. Soon afterward we began preparing for the winter's needs— hunting, killing, and seasoning wild game; driving to town for the winter's grubstake; dismantling the dude cabins and storing the bedding in rat-proof receptacles; and getting in the winter's wood. Before winter set in, this was sawed into stove and fireplace lengths, the splitting being saved for snappy days.

"Might as well let the weather lend a hand," Earl said once, as he demonstrated how much easier it was to split wood on a cold day.

It was uncanny the way these mountain men would forecast the weather. Early one afternoon, while we were visiting with Old Tex, Earl announced, "We'd better cut our visit short and hurry home before the storm."

"Why, Earl, the sun has been shining all morning," I remonstrated, reluctant to leave such good company in the middle of the day. "Just where do you hide your almanac?"

"If you keep your eyes and nose open, you don't need an almanac," he replied. "See those clouds above us floatin' at different levels in opposite directions? They're a sign of separate bodies of air at different temperatures, and that means a storm is brewin'. You'll notice also that the chimney smoke is fallin'. That means low pressure."

He had other signs, too, to forecast bad weather: birds flying low before a rain; swamps and ditches smelling stronger because low pressure permitted more gas to escape; some of the more sensitive wild flowers contracting their leaves at the approach of a storm; clouds settling low on the hills; and insects flying low because their wings were damp and heavy.

On the brighter side, clouds floated high in the air because they didn't have much moisture content; others dissolved as you watched them, meaning that the moisture was being taken up by the air and that good weather was in the offing. It was a good omen when the wind changed direction in the middle of a storm; and when we saw birds flying high and wheeling around and around before the wind, we knew that a breeze was not far off. Wind almost always brought a change for the better.

Wood operations required us to keep a team of horses in the fall, but Earl decided to have ours all winter. When I bemoaned the extra expense—baled hay had to be hauled in—his excuse was that he would need the horses to help place the logs for the new cabin he planned to build. But I knew the real reason was me; he wanted to be prepared in case I had to make a hurried trip to the hospital.

Traffic through Yellowstone Park was permitted as long after the season as Nature allowed. When snowplows had to be used, only the essential roads were cleared. We watched the road reports anxiously because we were expecting company from the park.

Denie, a savage friend from Old Faithful days who still spent her summers in the park, had stayed on late that fall and had promised to stop on her way out for a visit. Earl had met her the previous summer and had been favorably impressed, so we were hoping that she would like it well enough to stay all winter.

"It won't be much fun, being snowed in with a baby," Earl said. "You'll miss the ski trips over the trap line, so having company may help. Besides, what would you do if the baby got sick while I was away? It wouldn't do a bit of good to wring your hands and holler 'Earl.' Between the two of you, you ought to be able to tell whether he's cryin' from temper or colic."

"Maybe you've got something there," I replied.

I was glad she was coming for other reasons. This man's world was interesting, but there was nothing cozy about it. It would be wonderful to have the companionship of another girl. I missed Ma Crouch.

Mail day found me brittle with anticipation. During the fall the forest ranger made frequent trips up the river to mark timber for wood and house logs and repair the telephone line, and he always brought the upriver mail with him.

When the word finally came that Denie would be out the following Saturday on the last truck over Sylvan Pass, we were relieved, for we were worried lest she change her mind. We repaired, chinked, and redaubed the warmest of the cabins for her; and no dude was ever more warmly welcomed.

She was thrilled with the ranch and in no hurry to leave, having taken a year off from teaching. So far, everything was working out beautifully.

Because she liked to ride, I insisted upon her going with Earl whenever possible, for I couldn't go along any more, having at last outgrown my saddle. It was more fun to take Denie, anyway, for she was enthusiastic and given to superlatives.

Late one afternoon after a ride up the creek, Denie, convulsed with mirth, came limping into the kitchen. She looked generally disheveled, and there were several scratches across one cheek.

"What on earth happened to you?" I asked, as I filled the percolator and set the table for the lunch we always enjoyed after outdoor exercise.

"Well, all I can say is that silent husband of yours is certainly good company—can't even keep a girl awake. As we were riding along, the day was so quiet and the sun sifting through the pines so warm that I must have dozed off," she began.

"And you fell off Roany?" I prompted.

"Not exactly. I got pushed off, you might say." She giggled. "Your jack pines sure toss their branches around carelessly. There I was, riding along and minding my own business."

"Oh, Denie, get to the point."

"Well, as I said, I was riding along when I woke with a start to find a branch staring me in the face. I grabbed hold of it, expecting to break it off so I could go by. The darn thing wouldn't break, though. It just held me back, while Roany walked out from under me; and there I hung! I was scared to let go because the trail was so narrow, and I sure wasn't going to call Earl and let him find me like that! I dangled like a rag doll for a minute and *then* the branch broke. Down I tumbled, and I must have navigated half the hillside before a kind sapling stopped me."

She wasn't hurt, only scratched and bruised a little; but the episode furnished us amusement as we retold it, with many embellishments, to every cowboy and trapper who stopped in that winter.

It didn't take much to amuse us during those long,

isolated days. With nothing to do but live, we turned to simple pleasures and developed a profound interest in little things we had overlooked before. We had time to watch and smell and listen, and a new world was opened to us.

Every day we took a leisurely walk—doctor's orders for me—and every time we stepped outdoors we saw something new. We enjoyed tracking the artistic pattern of trails left by the little woodland animals. We examined the size and shape of each strange track, noting its spacing, then described our findings to Earl, who identified them. Generally we could only guess what the tracks revealed, but some of the stories in snow were easily interpreted. In one of these adventures the hero was a little pine squirrel who had tried to elude a hawk or eagle. Three times he successfully escaped his enemy, but on the fourth occasion he met with defeat. For several yards his tracks led straight toward a tree standing in a clearing. Suddenly the pattern changed to a melee of circles, figure eights and crossings; and scattered among the geometric figures the wing marks of a large bird were clearly seen. Then the tracks straightened out again and we imagined that the squirrel had decided to make a last run for the big pine tree.

The story ended in a clawed hollow in the snow, wing marks on either side disclosing the fact that the bird had won the battle. Not without a skirmish, however, for a few feet away from the hollow were tracks made by the tips of the bird's wings, with a dragging depression between, indicating trouble on the take off.

Denie and I were always raving about the beautiful white snow and were indignant when Earl scoffed.

"I was riding along dozing when I woke with a start to find a branch staring me in the face."

"When you've spent as many winters as I have shoveling off roofs and plowing through snowdrifts, it won't look so beautiful to you."

From the first tiny flurry of stinging snow which whirled through the air, patterning our windowpane with polka dots, we were intrigued. It was a strange sensation, finding in a little snowflake so much of interest. Just for fun we'd each take a window and, tracing the *moiré* patterns of the snowflakes on the panes, try to find duplicates of the small six-sided particles. Of course we never did, but it was a lesson in the beauty of form and design.

Once settled into the routine of winter, we ate only two meals a day, a late breakfast and an early supper. This left us long evenings to spend before the open fire, mainly in reading, for we had no radio bleating in our ears and teasing us to listen to murder mysteries or washboard weeps. Untrammeled by outside interests and with no part in the active drama of social life, reading took on a new importance; and the characters in the books seemed like living people.

A long winter in the wilderness can be a rewarding experience, especially if you share it with a kindred spirit. Aside from the spiritual value, you prove your self-sufficiency and find, to your surprise, that you are far tougher than you thought.

CHAPTER XXI

Too Much Roast Pig?

IN EARLY FALL we had an unexpected addition to the family, a gift from the forest ranger. Before presenting the yearling buck to us, the ranger admitted that he wasn't doing it to be nice.

"At the station, where people are coming and going all the time, a young deer is a plumb nuisance."

Before Earl could open his mouth to refuse, and I was sure he intended to, I implored in my most entreating voice, "Oh, Earl, I've never had a wild animal for a pet. Can't we please keep him?"

So, against Earl's better judgment, Spike was adopted. He was a friendly little fellow and made quite a picture with a red ribbon tied around his tiny horns, standing there beside the ranger.

"We've had him since he was a fawn," the ranger said. "I found him early last spring soon after his mother was killed by a coyote. This fall, come hunting season, we were afraid some hunter might shoot him so we tied the ribbon around his horns."

Spike took an immediate liking to Earl and followed him around like a dog. Starting out on a day's hunt, they made a curious pair, Earl with his red cap and

Spike with his matching ribbon; and it was a peculiar sight to look out the window at the end of the day and see a hunter limping wearily homeward, a full gun resting on his shoulder, an empty liver sack sticking out of his pocket, and a friendly young deer trotting along at his side. Spike looked well pleased with himself on such occasions.

We soon learned why he was considered a nuisance at the ranger station. His first misdemeanor was discovered when Denie went out to get the clean clothes from the line and found two dish towels in shreds.

"It must have been the wind," Earl defended, but he knew that the wind hadn't blown for several days, so the finger of guilt could point only to Spike.

At first we thought he was cute when he butted us with his little horns, but, as he waxed stronger, our amusement waned and soon he had Denie and me completely foiled. We were never sure when we stepped out the door whether we would complete our errand or have our minds changed for us and beat a hasty retreat. Just let Earl step off the place and we were held prisoners. One afternoon, while Earl was gone, we ran out of wood, so Denie volunteered to get an armload. Spike wasn't in sight as she walked bravely toward the woodpile; but before she reached it he came leaping from behind and stood there defiantly between her and the wood as if to say, "I dare you!" When Earl got home that night, he found us bundled up in our ski togs sitting before the stove, in which smouldered some half-charred magazines.

The climax came during one of Old Tex's infrequent visits. I was getting breakfast and looked out the window to see Old Tex playing with Spike. The next glance startled me for I saw something red drip from his hand. Then I knew Spike wasn't playing. I called Earl, and we rushed out to find that Spike had run his horn through the fleshy part of Old Tex's hand, between the thumb and forefinger. We all went back to the house while Earl dressed the wound, and then he announced, "Well, this has gone far enough. Before that deer hurts somebody seriously, we'll have to either shoot or dehorn him."

In spite of his bad behavior, Denie and I pleaded for the latter; so Earl, pleased with our decision, armed himself with a meat saw and we followed him outdoors. Spike brushed against him affectionately, and Earl grabbed both horns and threw him to the ground, as a cowboy bulldogs a steer.

"One of you girls sit on him and the other hold the off horn while I saw," he ordered.

Scared to death, we did as we were told. Spike squirmed and wiggled and kicked like a child having a temper tantrum. I never rode a bucking bronc, but after that it should be tame.

When both horns were sawed off, we turned him loose; and he ran into the timber where he remained until late that afternoon. When he returned he was a changed buck, cowed and humiliated. He ignored Denie and me. We were as unnoticed as the air we breathed, but Earl suffered a worse fate. Spike just looked at him with disappointed eyes, which, translated into deer language, accused, "How could you do this to me, your friend? Haven't we been buddies ever since I joined your family? How would you like it if I sneaked up and sheared your hair while a couple of my doe friends held you down? If that's what civilization does to a fellow, give me the wilderness every time."

Earl grumped around for several days, hating himself. When we tried to console him, he said, "Why didn't I shoot him? It would have been kinder. So help me, I hope somebody puts a bullet through my head if I ever do such a sneakin' low-down trick again."

When Spike saw Denie or me go toward the woodpile after that, he immediately leaped to cover. We missed him, and getting in the wood became just a monotonous chore instead of an adventure.

Two weeks later he disappeared into the forest, never to be seen again; and for days afterwards, an amoeba, a fungus, and a spore could have boasted more self-respect than we three.

"I hope nobody shoots him," Denie worried.

"I don't think anybody will," Earl said. "Hunting season is over, and by next season he'll grow a bigger set of horns and be able to look after himself."

"What do you mean he'll grow another set of horns?"

"That's the way nature takes care of the deer and elk," Earl answered, off on his favorite subject—game. "The fawns are born early in February, at which time the bucks shed their horns and start growin' another set. At first they look like small red tomatoes on each side of the forehead, full of nerves and very tender. For this reason the bucks take off into the timber and leave the does alone while they are raisin' their young. By the end of summer the horns have their full growth and are covered with furry hair. That's what we call 'in the velvet.' In early fall the horns set up an awful itchin' and the bucks horn the bushes for relief. In this way the velvet is brushed off and at the same time the horn is sharpened. Then next comes the matin' season when the bucks fight over the does."

"You said something about Spike's horns being bigger

next hunting season. Will he have another point every year?" Denie interrupted.

"No, not every year, but for the first four or five years they'll average about a point a year, if they've wintered good," Earl answered. "You seldom see a deer or elk with more than six points to a horn; and when you do, the extra points are generally due to some freak accident while the horns were in the velvet."

We were located in a good position to study wildlife, for we seldom stepped out of the yard without seeing some forest animal. Many of the open meadows on the sunny slopes of the mountains above us were blown clear of snow in winter and served as feeding grounds for deer and elk, while moose yarded up in the willow thickets along Gunbarrel Creek. Mountain sheep were frequently seen in the rocky crags of the highest peaks. Because they turn white in winter, they are hard to distinguish.

The work team paid for its feed in pleasure as well as in the work it saved. As soon as enough snow fell to insure good sledding, we enjoyed frequent sleigh rides, and drove to Yellowstone Park on Thanksgiving and ate dinner with the ranger and his wife, stopping en route to pick up Old Tex. The horse bells enhanced our gaiety; and the smooth road paved with packed snow lent itself easily to speed, so we quickly skimmed over the three miles between Old Tex's and the park. Dropping down a little hill through an avenue of fir trees, we found ourselves in a beautiful clearing, in the center of which stood the ranger station.

Those holiday dinners in the forest were outstanding events. We didn't see our neighbors often so we didn't have any petty annoyances to share. When we met, it was without the hangover of yesterday's argument or misunderstanding. We were so glad to see one another that we gave ourselves completely to the joy of companionship, tasting to the fullest the good cheer which comes from facing friends across the dining table.

Denie's presence added color to our holidays that year. She was as modern as today's newspaper, with the latest slang on the tip of her tongue; but she also had the good sense to keep still when silence was preferable. She was a person whom one invariably invites over and over again because she had a way of making all the other guests comfortable.

With a baby on the way, there wasn't any money to spend for Christmas presents so Denie and I made ours out of the scrap bag. We sewed Dutch aprons out of bleached flour sacks and trimmed them with bands of patchwork, using quilt blocks for patterns. They were fun to make, and each was an original. We also made pine-cone gardenias to send to our city friends. We cut the butt ends of limber pine cones— they look like flowers—and painted most of the scales white for petals and a few of the back ones green to resemble leaves. On the backs we fastened old overshoe hooks with powdered glue thickened with a little whiting. We smoothed them off; and when they were dry, they made attractive gardenia clips to set off a plain dress or blouse. I made Earl a bathrobe from an old blue army blanket, and raveled out an ill-fitting sweater and knitted a cap and scarf for Denie. Earl made a muff for me from the skin of a baby fawn he found dead in the forest, all that was left after some coyote had his dinner. That Christmas cost the least and meant the most of any we ever celebrated.

About a week before Christmas we drove up the

Paul Reeve Martin

I stayed with the horses while Denie and Earl scoured the hillsides for a perfect tree

wood road in the sled to get our tree; and I stayed with the horses while Denie and Earl scoured the hillsides on snowshoes hunting for a perfect one. It took several evenings for us to decorate it, for we made all the trimmings out of odds and ends we found around the ranch. Earl flattened an old tin can and cut a star for the top of the tree, and we strung yards and yards of popcorn for garlands. "Monkey Ward" furnished the candles and candleholders, and we splurged by sending for a ten-pound can of Christmas·candy. Under the tree was a bountiful supply of packages, many of them sent by dudes we had met the previous summer. We didn't open a single package until Christmas Eve, but we did as much shaking and pinching and guessing as small children.

Old Tex snowshoed down Christmas morning, and the four of us sat down to a dinner the like of which we had never eaten before and will probably never eat again. Since we couldn't afford a turkey, we decided to have an English Christmas and serve roast pig. It was no ordinary pig, either, but a very special variety sculptured from elk hamburger with an apple in its mouth. For a tail it had a bit of twisted juniper. Earl moulded it the day before, put it in the root cellar overnight, and baked it very slowly, so Mr. Yule Pig came out of the oven without even cracking his hide.

It was after dinner on Christmas Day that I began to feel a strange fluttering of foreboding which, try as I might, I couldn't argue down.

"I think maybe you had better take me to town," I whispered to Earl. "I've never felt like this before, so maybe we'd better not take any chances. It might be too much roast pig, but on the other hand——"

After one look at him, I took back everything I'd thought about his passive attitude. His face drained of color, and his voice was unsteady as he turned to Denie and instructed, "Denie, you call the station and ask the ranger to be all set to take us to the hospital, while I go and hitch up the team."

Old Tex offered to stay at the ranch with Denie while Earl was gone, so in a few minutes we were on our way. The horses were feeling their Christmas oats; it was a clear, still, warm day for December so sledding was excellent, and at five o'clock we were turning in at the ranger station. Two hours later I was in the hospital, being wheeled into the operating room for examination.

They then took me to my room and put me in a clean white bed—how cold the sheets felt compared to the flannel ones I was used to—and soon the doctor entered the room and addressed Earl and me.

"Are you particular about having your baby born on Christmas Day?"

Earl looked puzzled. "No, why do you ask?"

"We've been operating since nine o'clock this morning, and we're all pretty tired. Since your condition isn't urgent and the baby will have to be delivered by Caesarean section anyway, we'd rather wait until tomorrow morning for the operation and give the staff a chance to enjoy a little Christmas."

After he left the room, Earl turned to me and asked, "What did he mean—Caesarean section?"

"Oh," I said, feigning indifference, "he just means the baby can't be born; he'll be extracted."

"Isn't that serious?" he asked, concerned.

"Not particularly," I lied, "but it isn't every expectant mother who can put off the birthday of her offspring to a more convenient time or place."

It wasn't until Earl had left for the night that the gravity of my deception dawned on me, and I realized for the first time what a dreadful thing I had done. Ever since our visit to the doctor, I had known what to expect but had kept quiet for fear Earl would send me to town before Christmas. Why hadn't I told him the truth from the beginning? This might be the last impulsive act I'd perform, and just when I was beginning to see the light, and even reflect it a little!

And then I prayed, as I had never prayed before!

Next morning, when the operation was over, I regained consciousness with a troubled mind. Earl claims the first words I spoke were not the conventional "Is it a boy?" but that, instead, I whispered faintly, "Earl, will you take care of the gooseberry juice?"

He only smiled patiently, thinking me still delirious; and I had a bad time explaining to him that, on the day before Christmas, I'd opened a quart of the precious nectar and had used only a pint of it—that I wanted him to reseal the rest before it spoiled.

Later he confided, "Worried as I was, I was half-disgusted with you, lying there at death's door and stewing over a pint of wild gooseberry juice!"

CHAPTER XXII

Forty-Two Below

MOTHER SENT ME a baby manual, so I started out raising our son "according to the book." No child of mine would ever be kept up after bedtime and no candy would ever pass his lips to rot his potential molars!

Earl, Junior, wasn't two months old, however, before he started oozing out the margins of the book, and I was forced to make one concession and then another. The climax came when Earl took him on his lap and fed him a bit of hot cake drenched in syrup and butter. He liked it, too, and, chip off the old block, has been eating undigestible hot cakes ever since.

Earl built a little covered-wagon sled into which his basket fitted, so at an early age Buckshot—horrible nickname for an innocent babe—was initiated into the mysteries of the forest. As soon as I was able to exercise, Denie and I bundled him up in his basket, set it in his prairie schooner, and off we went on skis, dragging the sled behind us.

A tiny baby who stayed put wasn't much care; it was when he reached the wiggly stage that problems arose—for instance, what to do about floors with splinters.

Weather permitting, we often laid young Buckshot down in the middle of our bed and let him kick. One afternoon I left him and went to the kitchen to bake a cake for supper. It must have been a half an hour later when I returned to find the bed empty. Having heard Denie come in and then go out again, I supposed that she had taken him to her cabin. I stepped to the door and called, and when she said she didn't have him, I rushed frantically back to the living room to search. He had rolled off the bed and against the far wall where he was fast asleep on the hard floor.

Remembering the nightmare I had that night still makes me break out in a cold sweat. I dreamed that he had rolled under the bed, just as he actually had, only in the dream he was full of splinters when I found him. When I jerked them out, I discovered that I had pulled out all his ribs! After that Earl made a play pen for him, and later, when he began to crawl, a walker, copied from a picture in the catalog.

A young mother who must raise her baby miles away from a doctor faces many terrifying experiences, not the least of which is croup. I was alone when he had his first attack. He woke up from his nap with a start, choking and gasping for breath. I grabbed him from his crib, shaking and patting him vigorously, but he only coughed harder. I warmed some water but he wouldn't take it. In desperation I rushed to the telephone and tried to call the doctor. I rang again and again but central didn't answer. Finally a voice asked, "Are you trying to get town?"

"Yes, it's an emergency."

"Nobody's been able to get town all day. Can I help you?"

I poured out my troubles to the lady who had once owned the cuckoo clock.

"Now, don't you worry, honey; he's only got the croup. Jest you get a pan of water boiling and put a teaspoonful of creosote or carbolic salve in it and set it near the baby's head. Then stretch a sheet over him and the pan, tentwise, an' he'll soon be breathin' natural again." It worked, and never again was I to complain about folks who listen in over party lines.

Icing was one of the main events on our winter's program, all the families of the upper river pooling their man power and sleds and other equipment. The park ranger was the first to put his up, and then the crew moved on down the river, ending at Blackwater, four miles below us.

Had it not been for Denie, Earl could not have helped that winter; but with a well-stocked woodpile and the water hole near by, we insisted upon his joining the crew, assuring him that we wouldn't be afraid.

In our country, perfect icing weather was scarce; so when it came, all other activities stopped and woodsmen "parked their axes in mid-air" to rush to the river. Each rancher had his private pond in the river which he watched carefully, measuring the ice until it was at least sixteen inches, the best thickness for cutting and packing. If the weather turned warm, the ice couldn't be cut lest the warm wind honeycomb the cut-off chunks before they would be packed into the icehouse, so icing weather was necessarily cold weather. Ice couldn't be too thick, either, or it would be too hard to saw; and it must be located in a pool deep enough to allow sufficient unfrozen water beneath to give play for the saw. The men took turns at the saw; and when a load was ready, the chunks were pulled out with ice tongs, loaded into the bobsleds, and hauled to the icehouse. Packing was a "know-how" job, for unless every air space between the blocks was filled with ice or sawdust, the ice would start melting on the first hot day. As the layers built up, the packing became backbreaking labor because there was so little room in which to work. Finally, over the top went all the remaining sawdust, leaving an air space between it and the roof.

When the icing operations got down as far as Timber Lodge, Earl rode one of the horses back and forth. On what he supposed would be the last day of icing there, I suggested, "Why don't you ski up this morning and let Denie ride the horse; then you can both bring the sled back tonight. It will be fun for her, and I don't mind being alone with the baby for a day."

It wasn't too cold when they left, but when I made my mid-morning pilgrimage to the thermometer, the temperature had fallen to twenty below zero. The air was biting and my hand, still damp from dishwashing, stuck to the doorknob.

The house seemed draftier than usual that morning, so I didn't give the baby a bath. While he was sleeping I warmed up some soup and pulled my chair closer to the fire to eat my lunch. It was about one-thirty when the phone rang and Denie said, "Now, don't be upset. He's all right, but Earl fell in the river this afternoon."

"In the river? He must be frozen!" I exclaimed in alarm.

"It's twenty-five below now. Earl's clothes froze into a windbreak immediately, which is probably what saved him. He ran all the way up from the river, has changed into dry clothes, and is toasting by the fire.

When a load was ready, the chunks were loaded on the bobsled and hauled to the icehouse.

He says to tell you he may be late getting home this afternoon. Doesn't dare start out until he's sure he has thawed out."

"Please don't come until you are sure he is O.K.," I said, and added, "Did you get through icing?"

"No," she answered, "Earl will have to come back tomorrow. It's too cold to work this afternoon and it will take another half day to finish."

She hung up before I thought of the inconvenience of their coming home that night just to keep me company. I finally mustered enough courage to call her back and say, "Denie, everything is fine here. I've been keeping the wood box full from the pile on the porch; Buckshot has been a perfect angel all day; and I'm not in the least afraid, so why don't you stay there for the night and come back tomorrow when the job is finished?"

The receiver was scarcely back on its hook before I started feeling sanctimonious, as though I had given my last crust to a beggar, or thrown the suspicion of the law on myself to protect a friend. Maybe staying alone in the wilderness on a night like this wouldn't put me in line for a Carnegie medal, but it had certainly taken all the courage I had to suggest it.

The afternoon passed slowly, but I huddled close to the fire and gave myself pep talks. It was with the deepening shadows that loneliness came. When the phone rang, I jumped out of my chair.

It was Earl on the line saying, "Throw another chunk of wood on the fire. It's forty-two below."

Forty-two below zero! My blood practically congealed at the thought. I looked appraisingly at the wood box and decided to go out for more wood before it got colder. Although the woodpile was only a few steps from the door, I bundled up in coat and cap and mittens. As I stepped outside, the snow underfoot was hard and crackled like walking on popcorn. Looking up, I stood for a moment spellbound by the pageantry of the starlit sky. The air was crystal clear, and the dancing stars overhead were so bright that the white mountains glittered in their radiance.

As I entered with the second load of wood, the phone rang again. It wasn't our ring, but I listened anyway—maybe hearing a human voice would make me warmer. Two women, whose voices I couldn't identify, were talking and one of them was saying, "I wouldn't want to be in her shoes tonight—all alone way up there in that Godforsaken canyon. She could freeze to death and nobody'd be the wiser—and with a new baby, too!"

I thought to myself, "That poor woman"—and then I realized they were talking about me! I replaced the receiver guiltily, feeling lonelier and colder than ever.

There wasn't a breath of air stirring outside, but the house logs creaked like reports from a six-gun; and a pack of coyotes up the draw "howled out their woes to the homeless snows," adding their lonesome bit to the frozen night's symphony. I was grateful for the company of Ring until he howled back at the coyotes and frightened me almost out of my wits. Once I heard a noise outside and imagined it must be a moose, and it was a little comforting to think that there was something else as lonely and cold as I.

It was impossible to settle down. I'd read a few lines of a story and then drop my magazine to go out to the kitchen and stuff Virginia; I'd start a game of solitaire and leave it to throw another log in the fireplace; I'd go to the desk and start a letter home only to abandon it and put more wood in the heater. I must have burned a week's supply of wood in that one night.

Even knitting couldn't compose my nerves. For every knit-two purl-two, I'd drop four. I'd just succeed in getting my mind settled when either the logs would pop or the coyotes set up their dirge again. It was no use; I might as well give up and go to bed.

After filling hot-water bottles and warming bricks for our beds, I reversed the usual procedure and dressed for bed. I put on plenty! Over my long underwear I slipped a long-sleeved flannel nightgown, and on top of that a loose warm sweater. A pair of Earl's lumberjack socks were the last addition, and I must have looked like a stuffed teddy bear as I crawled into bed.

I slept fitfully and the telephone conversation haunted me. I kept thinking, "I don't dare go to sleep. The fires might go out and Earl, Jr., would freeze in his sleep." I would check the stoves only to find them so full they couldn't hold another stick. Then I'd pile more logs in the fireplace. Then I decided it would be better to take Buckshot in bed with me; and, having made the transfer, I lay there worrying for fear I'd go to sleep and suffocate him under the covers. I must have gotten up a dozen times to attend to the fires; and when dawn came I added "longest" to the adjectives describing that dreadful night.

When Earl called that morning I bit my lip to keep from telling him how lonely I had been and how long the night seemed. Instead, I said, "Everything is fine, so don't hurry home on my account."

I was sure proud of myself, but privately I wondered how long it would be after he got home before I blatted out the whole story and spoiled my record. However,

Earl beat me to the draw by saying, "It was swell of you to suggest that we stay. I dreaded goin' out in the cold after my soakin'. I'm sure glad you didn't get cold or lonesome. I was worried that you would."

After such a build-up, how could I possibly play the martyr?

CHAPTER XXIII

Family Growing Pains

DURING PROHIBITION the most flourishing business on the river was that of Seth, the local moonshiner—the Daniel Boone of my first schoolhouse dance. As with other issues, my opinion of moonshining was also changing. While I didn't approve of the business, wasn't it better to drink his good whisky than some of the poisonous stuff bootlegged in?

Tales of Seth's adventures in outwitting the law made good listening, and no one could spin these yarns better than Old Tex.

"When I first come to the river," he told us, "Seth wuz playin' a cat an' mouse game with the law; but not carin' fer cheese, he never took their bait.

"One day the law got wind that he wuz gone an' come to his place with a search warrant. Seth's wife wuz real nice an' took the officer through the house, but he never found nuthin'. As he was leavin', I reckon he got to thinkin' that it wuz a sorry dog that didn't bury a bone somewheres, so he went back in the house fer another look. On a hunch he crawled under the bed, an' sure enuff, back in a dark corner he found a gallon jug. Jest to make sure, he lifts up the jug an' takes a swig. It was hardly down before he starts frothin' at the mouth an' cryin' fer help. He wuz already turnin' purple when Seth's wife got to him; an' when she found out what he'd done, she run to the kitchen fer a couple of eggs an' some milk, an' poured it down his throat. He laid there on the floor fer quite a spell before he finally snapped out of it. I reckon that killin' dose of formaldehyde learned him not to go snoopin' around, drinkin' outa strange bottles no more. Seth's wife wuz a kind lady an' she wuz sure sorry about the accident.

" 'We keep it back there so nobody will drink it by mistake,' she explained."

Unwittingly we found ourselves a party to one of Seth's capers.

It was early spring, and Earl was in the timber getting out fireplace wood when a phone message came from the rancher down country who was pasturing our horses that winter.

"Your horses!" he began excitedly. "The sheriff came and got 'em."

"The sheriff?" I yelped. "What on earth does the sheriff want with our horses? Did they get into somebody's hay?"

In a rush of words, he told me the sheriff, having at last discovered the hiding place of Seth's still, had seized our outfit to pack out the supplies, which included two tons of sugar.

The pack outfit didn't get back to the ranch till late that evening, so they stored the sugar in the rancher's chicken coop, planning to truck it into town the next day. We learned, via the party line, that when the law came back for their "sweetnin" next morning it was gone. Seth had stolen his own sugar back.

Though the sheriff ranted and raved, no one ever saw the sugar again. Since the raid served only as a recess for his business, Seth no doubt used it to make more moonshine.

We thought the incident was closed, and it never occurred to us that there would be any bad feeling; but according to the grapevine, Seth considered it a personal affront. When the rumor reached us it had grown into "Seth says he's out to get Earl the next time they meet."

I was frightened to death, and while Earl appeared calm, I could tell that the threat bothered him, too. All of a sudden the spring dance to which we had looked forward all winter lost its attraction. I kept the reason from Denie and tried to persuade her and Earl not to go.

"What shall we do with Buckshot?" I asked, feeling that here at last was an excuse for staying home.

"Take him along," Earl answered. "We can put him to bed in his basket and set it on the back seat. We'd better take that little Sterno stove to heat his bottle if he wakes up."

So it was settled—we would go to the dance. What a pilgrimage! A twenty-five-mile drive over rough mountain roads and through snowbanks, in an old-fashioned car with curtains flapping in the breeze and a four-months-old baby asleep on the back seat!

On this, my second schoolhouse dance, I noticed a change in the atmosphere. While the neighbors didn't wholeheartedly accept me, at least they treated me like a shirttail relative; and the women didn't deliberately change the subject when they saw me coming. Having a baby in a basket no doubt raised my social status. Had it not been for my secret fear that this might be the night chosen by Seth "to get Earl," the dance would have been fun.

I kept my eagle eye focused on the door, hoping that Seth wouldn't come to the dance, but he finally arrived. From that time on, I danced a straight program with Earl, afraid to let him out of my sight.

The climax came just after lunch. Seth sauntered across the dance floor, greeted us both, and then asked Earl to step out to his car. Earl excused himself and followed Seth while I sat glued to the seat, feeling the blood drain from my face and my knees turn to wet sponges. Six months before, I probably would have rushed impetuously after him, but now something held me back. No matter what happened, I couldn't risk destroying Earl's self-respect. The blood of frontiersmen, who settled disputes with guns, flowed in his veins; and while he would never provoke a fight, he wouldn't run away from trouble or hide behind a woman's petticoats.

Weak from fear and half expecting to hear a pistol shot in the night, I sagged back on the bench. The next five minutes seemed like eternity. Terror held me so tightly in its grip and imagination lowered me to such depths that when I looked up to see Earl and Seth standing beside me, I was startled to the point of embarrassment. Seth remarked gallantly, "Are you ill, Mrs. Martin? Perhaps you'd like a drink, too."

It took only a moment to regain composure, and the blissful feeling of relief to learn that all was well between them was almost worth the anguish. There was a crowd around us then; but during the after-supper dance, Earl said, "I don't mind admitting that I'm glad that's over."

"Oh, Earl, what did he say? Did he threaten you?"

"Funny thing. He never even mentioned the raid. Just asked me to have a drink and talked about the weather. Guess his threat was only gossip."

For the rest of the evening I danced as the Indian dances, for the sheer joy of expression, and could have gone on dancing to the end of time. The baby woke up once, in the middle of a quadrille, but it was Denie who warmed his bottle. Earl was the center of my attention; this was his night!

We were among the last to leave and were surprised to step out into a miniature blizzard. We declined an invitation to spend the night at a near-by ranch and, facing the storm like a buffalo, headed up the river toward home. It was slow going for we had no wiper; so whenever the windshield snowed over, we had to stop and wipe it off with an old glove. At Newton Creek, three miles from home, we started bucking snowdrifts; and Earl shoveled our way at intervals for the last two miles.

Midway through one of the largest drifts, Buckshot woke up with a lusty howl. It wasn't bottle time, but we were too tired to argue with him. We set up the Sterno and began to heat his bottle. All of a sudden we realized what a ridiculous picture we made —crouched in the back seat, huddled over that tiny stove and heating formula for a four-months-old tyrant, while outside the storm swirled around Earl and his shovel. We burst into loud giggles, much to Earl's disgust. With sweat rolling down his cheeks and every breath a frosty puff, he didn't see anything funny.

April must have missed our griping that spring, for we were far too worried to pay attention to the weather. Earl, Jr., was teething, had no appetite, and was losing weight. When all remedies in the book and suggestions from the party line failed, we decided to take him to town to a doctor, poor roads or no.

According to river custom, we had errands to run for several families. There were groceries for Old Tex as well as the ranger and ourselves, crochet thread to match for the postmaster's wife, and school supplies for the teacher. We were looking forward to a busy day.

Our first stop was at the doctor's, who prescribed, of all things, goat's milk. We left Buckshot at Aunt Ruby's (my nurse when he was born) and Denie and I hurried around town doing the shopping while Earl went goat hunting.

It was four o'clock before he found a goat and appeared at Ruby's to take us home. He didn't say anything; but we could tell by the glint in his eyes that he'd been up to something; so we weren't too surprised to find a strange car parked in front of the house.

"I traded off Willy for this Dodge Commercial," he explained. "With two wives, a baby, and now a goat, I decided we'd need more room. We can lug anything around in this."

One peek in the back convinced us that "everything" was a better word. Behind the front seat there was barely enough space left to accommodate the baby basket. Once in, it was wedged into place by sacks of potatoes, a hundred-pound bag of sugar, ax handles, boxes of groceries, and other paraphernalia. Behind, and separating the "nursery" from the "stable," were three bales of alfalfa hay, back of which the goat was tied with only room to inhale.

All went well until we were about halfway up what we familiarly called the "Dam Hill," the most hazardous ascent in the canyon. Earl shifted gears as he always did, but instead of climbing, we shot backwards, down the hill. Earl slammed on the brakes and steered the car toward the canyon wall. Bang! We stopped with a terrific jolt, the three of us wedged against the door. Earl had forgotten that the Dodge didn't have a standard gearshift.

Such confusion! The baby was crying and the goat was bleating. Fortunately, nobody was hurt, but never have I seen such a shambles. Buckshot had been thrown out of his basket and was squirming and howling at the feet of the goat which was too frightened to do anything but tremble. One of the potato sacks had ripped open, and spuds were scattered all over the back of the car. Groceries lodged in every corner. One suit of new underwear dangled from an ax handle.

Denie and I looked up, caught each other's eye, and burst out laughing.

"I'd never risk taking you two girls to a wake," Earl said sarcastically. "You'd probably have convulsions."

We restored some semblance of order to our "commissary," and snickering admonitions about the new gearshift, proceeded on our way.

At each delivery stop, the goat, which we had already named Newt, short for Nutrition, was displayed; and of course we had to tell everybody about our adventure. It was almost suppertime when we neared the Trail Shop, our local post office, and the halfway mark between town and Gunbarrel Creek.

"We'll just about make it to the Trail Shop in time for supper," Earl remarked.

It was Denie who remonstrated, "Aren't we stretching our welcome a bit—three of us dropping in at mealtime without an invitation?"

Nobody was hurt, but never have I seen such a shambles

"I know exactly how you feel, Denie," I answered. "It wasn't so very long ago when I asked the same question, and Earl told me just what I am telling you now, 'Oh, they'll just throw in an extra potato.'"

CHAPTER XXIV

The Mechanics of Dude Ranching

SYLVAN PASS was our spring barometer. When the work
of clearing snow was started, we knew the dude season
wasn't far behind. From the East Entrance of Yellowstone Park, the road spirals for seven miles to the top
of the 8,650-foot pass, which fills completely with ice
and snow during the winter. Every spring a railroad
representative and a park official drove to Timber Lodge
and stayed overnight, proceeding by car as far as possible the next morning and finishing the trip to the
top of the pass on snowshoes. Here a couple of park
rangers met them from the other side, and the four
held a powwow to decide when the snow would be
blasted and shoveled out. There were, of course, no
snowplows then to make the clearing easy.

At the appointed time, crews started working from
both ends, tunneling through the snowbanks to make
a trail just wide enough for one car. Until the snow
melted weeks later, one-way travel only was permitted,
flagmen being stationed at both ends to alternate the
procession. While travelers waited their turns, many
snowball fights were staged.

An epidemic of house cleaning swept the valley as

the ranchers prepared for the coming of the dudes. Besides the routine jobs of cleaning cabins, airing blankets, and moving beds to accommodate the size of the parties, some of the cabins had to be redaubed. Most of them were made of logs and chinked inside with small poles, but outside the cracks were filled with a mixture of gravel, cement, and sawdust. The temperature changes of the winter often caused chunks of this material to fall out and it had to be replaced. In addition to the beds and a dresser, each room was furnished with a writing table and a washstand, the latter equipped with a washbowl, pitcher, and duck (our word for chamber). Then, of course, there was the ever-present kerosene lamp—the bane of my existence!

While the women were busy with these chores, the men found plenty to do, too. Summer plumbing was overhauled; the water supply tank was cleaned out; and the corrals and grounds cleared of winter debris. They faced another big task—that of driving the horses from winter pastures to summer grazing on forest meadows, and besides, each one had to be shod. Then each horse was ridden out, for no fractious animal was ever assigned to a guest. Oh, it was a big time of year for all of us!

Most of our dudes were booked through correspondence, the chief supply coming from satisfied guests who told their friends about the good times they had had last summer. The railroad helped, too, by publishing a brochure with information about every ranch reached via their line. Some of the more opulent ranchers went east every spring and contacted prospective guests personally.

The many advantages of a ranch vacation were stressed. Where else can you go without spending tiresome hours shopping for clothes, without discarding old ones because they are out of style? Most of the dudes buy their ranch clothes upon their arrival at the Western town nearest the ranch. Local merchants are well supplied with every need and the outfits often cost less than in the city. The same jeans and shirts can be worn year after year. Dudes look pretty much alike in Western clothes, except that they stick out in different places.

Once a party of four stopped in town on their way out to the ranch and spent a small fortune on Western regalia. The men even bought the most expensive chaps they could find. Not one of them rode a horse more than twice during their two-weeks stay. They preferred to dress up in their new riding clothes, sit in the living room, and play bridge. When Earl sputtered to me about them, I said, "I can't see why you are so upset. They don't give you nearly as much trouble as they would if they rode. They're having a good time, so why worry?"

"Well," he replied, "it looks stupid to me, paying out good money to sit around all day and play cards. They might as well have stayed home for all the good their vacation's doin' 'em."

There is no keeping up with the Joneses on a dude ranch. Here your popularity is in no way dependent upon your bankroll. If you are a good camper, agreeable to others, and thoughtful of their needs, you are bound to be popular; if not, your good looks, style, antecedents, or social standing back home will avail you little.

When we first started dude ranching, most of the guests arrived by rail and were met in Cody by the ranch owner. After shopping, they drove out to the ranch and got settled in their cabin for the night, travel-weary from the long trek across the country in a Pullman. Now they are apt to stop in town for the nightly performance of the "pup rodeo," sponsored by the local saddle club. The riders are the cowboys from the surrounding outfits, and often the dudes take part in square dancing on horseback and other riding games. Together, they put on a really good show.

Supposing you, the reader, have just arrived for your first ranch vacation. After the best rest you can remember, you eat a hearty breakfast at a long ranch table and hurry with the others to the corral. Here is the core of the ranch. You await your turn to be assigned a horse. Regardless of your experience, the guide always starts you out with a gentle animal; and your progress from "nag" to "spirited mount" is determined by your ability to handle your horse, not by what you tell the guide you know.

A saddle is then selected to fit you, the stirrups adjusted to your legs, a few instructions issued, and off you go on your first morning's ride. If you are smart, you'll disregard the ensuing stiffness and ride again that afternoon; in a day or two you will be seasoned for an all-day trip. It's as easy as that!

Dude ranching is especially recommended for families. On a ranch, old and young can mingle and have fun doing the same things. Very gentle horses are provided for the children, and every ranch has a shallow stream where the children can wade and play in the dirt or sand while the parents rest and visit in comfortable chairs. Children may forget what they have read or been told about nature, but lessons learned along a mountain trail stay with them always.

The fish and game commissions keep the creeks well

What fun we all had at those chummy little rodeos

stocked with fish, and the ranch cook is always willing
to fry a day's catch for a fisherman, especially if there
is one left for her.

We often took our dudes to visit neighboring ranches.
Some outfits discouraged this practice for fear the dudes
would make comparisons and maybe go to the other
place next year; but Earl reacted characteristically, "If
they like it better somewhere else, we don't want 'em
here."

Evenings were generally spent in the ranch living
room, the guests reading, writing letters, or visiting
before an open fire. Occasionally an evening of silly
amateur theatricals was staged, and we had fun teaching the dudes how to square dance. About twice a
summer we had a masquerade, costumes concocted from
things we found around the ranch. Anything in the
way of good clean fun was encouraged.

Several Sunday afternoons found the cowboys from
Timber Lodge and neighboring ranches staging a rodeo
on the flats near the river and close to the main road.
Bleachers were fallen logs, and the arena was the open
meadow. Yellow busses en route for the park would
stop for a few minutes to witness the show. When
the crowd was at its peak, one of the dudes was sure
to pass the hat to the spectators; and the money would
later be divided among the riders. Once the collection
amounted to over ninety dollars. The main bucking
horse was Guts, who was kept expressly for that purpose. He wasn't safe to ride for pleasure. What fun
we all had at those chummy little rodeos.

We didn't ride on Sunday. After a full week, the
horses really needed a day of rest. Because the cars
of that time weren't geared to speed, we seldom drove
the forty miles to church. Sometimes a visiting min-

ister would drive out to the schoolhouse where we would assemble for worship. When I bemoaned these circumstances, Earl quoted from one of his favorite poems:

> Oh, Lord, I never lived where churches grow,
>   I love creation better as it stood
> That day You finished it so long ago
>   And looked upon Your work and called it good.
> I know that others find You in the light
>   That's sifted down through tinted windowpanes,
> And yet I seem to feel You near tonight
>   In the dim quiet starlight of the plains.

How right he was. Our church spires were the rocky pinnacles which rose from the canyon floor; our choir was the music of the water and the soft sound of breezes sifting through pine needles, our prayer the reverent silence of the forest. Surely God must be very near!

Chapter XXV

Dudes—

WE LOOKED FORWARD to the coming of the dudes in summer as a child does to Christmas, and we were as glad in the fall when the last guest had departed and we could take our hair down and indulge in a spell of bad disposition, as a family sometimes does after New Year's Day when the decorations are all cleared away and life settles down to C major again.

Since ours was one of the smaller and less pretentious dude ranches, we were spared the ordeal of entertaining the rich society class, the type that has been everywhere and seen everything, that prefers strong drink to wholesome food and demands a lot of individual attention.

Our guest list was made up largely of two classes of vacationers: families of business and professional men who were too busy to spare more than a month for a holiday, and young people holding clerical positions who rated only a two- or three-weeks vacation and wanted to cram it as full as possible. While the latter exhausted us, they made delightful guests for they were generally thrilled with everything. This type rose with the dawn, took turns helping the wrangler bring in the horses in the morning, and were the last to go to bed. They must have returned to their jobs physically exhausted, for they never rested. Many of them came back summer after summer, bringing friends with them, until we grew so personally interested that on the day of reckoning one of us would fade out, leaving the other to make up the bill because we felt like we were charging friends for paying us a visit.

The many and varied responsibilities of a ranch hostess weighed heavily upon me that summer, and by the end of the season I knew what Ma Crouch meant when she said, "Don't take it too much to heart when the dudes look at you enviously and say, 'How romantic! I'd simply a-d-o-r-e being a hostess on a dude ranch.' I grant it's interesting, but you don't have much fun yourself. You are supposed to make it fun for them, and, believe me, it's no mean job."

After my first year in that capacity, I felt qualified for the diplomatic service. Sometimes it ballooned into a Herculean task, trying to please everybody at the same time, for, while nature in the raw was the doctor's orders for some, others preferred their Western atmosphere strained and whipped up into a soufflé.

Because the ranch was small and the dudes and roughnecks were thrown closely together, we hired only the better class of help, for it was not uncommon for an attractive dudine to fall madly in love with the chore boy or for some dashing widow to swoon at the sight of the horse wrangler.

While most of these affairs were only summer romances, some of them led to the altar. As I watched one blossom, I worried to Earl, "Don't you think we ought to write to Betty's mother and suggest she send for her to come home? It would be dreadful if she and Slim got married."

Betty was an attractive young lady, educated at a finishing school in Paris, while Slim was a typical cowboy, carefree, lovable and irresponsible, and almost every bone in his body had been broken during his career as a rodeo rider.

"Of course not," was Earl's reply. "She's old enough to know what she's doin'. Besides, I don't see anything so terrible about a dudine marryin' a cowboy. You roped one yourself, didn't you?"

"Yes, but I wasn't a rich dudine," I defended. "I was a park savage, and that makes a difference."

"Oh, it does, does it?" I didn't miss the twinkle in his eye.

Even after their runaway marriage, I continued to worry, and prophesied pessimistically with others, "It won't last six months."

That was twenty-five years ago, and they are still happily married, she having successfully adjusted her life to his.

In a second case my concern was with the roughneck rather than the dudine. Hank was a Southerner, slow, easygoing and good-natured, with a drawl that, on occasion, could stretch clear from Wyoming to Texas. He drifted in that fall and worked for us through hunting season, then stayed the winter, doing chores for his board and tobacco money.

Hank could do anything and do it willingly. He liked to take care of babies and his soft, soothing voice would lull Buckshot to sleep when nothing else would. If he saw dirty dishes in the sink he'd wash them, and it was uncanny the way he always showed up when needed. His only shortcoming was carelessness about his person. His outside clothes always looked clean; but after a couple of weeks I noticed an unpleasant odor and, since Earl refused to say anything about it, summoned enough courage to suggest one night after supper, "Hank, after I get the dishes washed, why don't you fill a tub with water and heat it for a bath? I hate to say anything, but you need one so badly that you smell."

Earl stalked from the room in disgust, but Hank only smiled at me and drawled, "Now, don't you-all feel bad about tellin' me that. Ah figger if a feller needs a bath so bad he smells, an' he cain't smell hisse'f, somebody oughta tell him."

After that all I had to say was, "Well, Hank, tonight's bath night," and the charm of cleanliness was added to his other virtues.

Hank was in the forest snaking out house logs when Miss Shultz arrived. She had written smoothly that she wanted to come out in winter to "absorb atmosphere and write." I could hardly wait to see what she was like, picturing her as an attractive young woman with personality plus. Was I surprised! She was scrawny and awkward and had barely enough chin to hold up her face. She looked like a whitefish and had the deep voice of a bullfrog.

Neither for business nor diplomacy could Earl be forced to pretence. He either liked a person or he didn't; and from the very first Miss Shultz was repulsive to him. I spread a lot of axle grease and peach butter that winter trying to keep peace in the family. Fortunately, she spent most of her time in her cabin; but the meals were often tense with her insistent advances and Earl's apparent repugnance. She confided to me, "Earl only *thinks* he dislikes me. We were both born under the same star and should be attracted to each other, for our auras blend perfectly. Just give him time, and he'll come around."

When the days stretched into weeks, the weeks into months, and he hadn't shown any signs of "coming around," she called him into her cabin one morning and inquired, "Earl, I've tried for five months to make you like me, but you are still as cold as ice. Why aren't you nicer to me?"

When he told me about it afterward, he said that he was so surprised that he couldn't think of an answer, so he countered in embarrassment, "What do you expect me to do, Miss Shultz, take you in my arms whenever we meet at breakfast?"

She simpered, "You wouldn't care to, would you?"

Completely sickened, he replied, "You're damned right, I wouldn't!" He slammed the door behind him.

After that we decided that neither her money nor our reputation for satisfied guests was worth the effort. We concentrated on making her mad enough to go home.

She stayed on, though, for another month, focusing her wiles on Hank. At first he took it as a joke when we teased him about her; but they kept getting thicker and thicker, and one spring day they disappeared. We learned they had gone to Billings to be married and later moved to California, where she was leading him around by the nose and he was again working for his board and tobacco. Poor Hank, he was such a good egg!

A cowboy is the most democratic person on earth. In his eyes, people are all alike whether they come from Nob Hill or the Bowery.

One day we received a letter from some dudes who

had been guests at the ranch when the Crouches were there. They wanted reservations for some friends of theirs.

I almost swooned.

"The Cabots! Oh, Earl, not them!"

"What's the matter with the Cabots?" he wanted to know. "Do they have something catching?"

"It isn't that," I answered. "It's just that we aren't swanky enough to entertain *the Cabots from Boston.*"

He didn't know the Cabots and had never heard the famous limerick about them, so I quoted it for him:

> Boston, beautiful Boston,
> Land of the baked bean and cod,
> Where the Cabots speak only to Lowells,
> And the Lowells speak only to God.

Earl wasn't impressed. "I wouldn't worry about it if I were you. Just treat 'em like you would the Joneses of Pumpkin Center. Chances are they're coming West to get away from all that swank anyway. If they don't like us as we are, they can always leave."

I didn't go with him to meet them. I wanted everything to be just right so I stayed to attend to last-minute details.

They ate supper in town, so it was well past nine when the car drove into the lane. They were so tired and travel-weary that they went right to their cabin.

Next morning after breakfast, Mrs. Cabot asked, "Do you have a washtub I could borrow?"

"Why, yes, of course," I answered, "but what do you plan to do with a washtub?"

"We both feel dirty after our trip, so I'm going to have my husband fill a tub with creek water and we can warm it on our stove for baths."

"But we have a bathhouse," I protested.

"Don't tell me you have a bathhouse! How grand! The place in Maine where we often spend our vacations hasn't any conveniences, so we didn't expect to find any out here in the Rockies."

And that wasn't all. Her husband chopped all the wood they used in their cabin and she made their own beds and kept the room cleaned up!

I always think of her on ironing day for she was responsible for a reform which has saved me lots of work through the years.

I was ironing sheets when she stepped into the kitchen to get a drink, and suggested, "Why do you iron them? They smell so sweet and clean when taken from the line that I always have them put back on the beds without ironing."

"Well," I said to myself, "if the Cabots from Boston can sleep on unironed sheets, the Martins from Gunbarrel surely can." From that day to this, I've never ironed another sheet.

Of course we had our share of funny guests, both "funny-peculiar" and "funny-ha-ha." They added spice to our bill of fare.

There was Miss Lane, a sentimental old maid, who followed me into the kitchen after her first meal, and complained, "I'm very much disappointed, Mrs. Martin. I expected to find a lot of gentlemen guests, and there isn't a single unattached male here."

She perked up when I told her that three bachelors were expected on the following Saturday.

"Oh," she said, "that will be much better. You see I am the type who is more attractive to men than to women, so I always have a better time in masculine society."

At the corral, where the guests assembled for the morning's ride, she turned to Earl and announced, making sure that all the others were within earshot, "Now you needn't be afraid to give me one of the more spirited mounts, for I've ridden horses all my life. If I do say it myself, there isn't much I don't know about them. You see, my grandfather was a breeder of Kentucky race horses."

That was the only hint Earl needed to start her out on Badger, who was the smartest horse we had. He'd take care of her—horse-wise or horse-foolish. Had her request been granted, I doubt that she would have gotten out of the barnyard, once the "spirited mount" got a squint at her riding habit.

She wore "chokeboard" trousers with wrap-around leggings, but her high-heeled kid pumps left a two-inch margin of silk stocking exposed. A black-and-white checked jacket was the only "horsey" garment she had on, and it looked nice in spite of the lacey jabot that stuck out between the lapels. It was her hat that really set her costume off—a large, floppy picture hat with a wreath of red poppies around the crown. She wore it anchored to her head by a filmy gray veil, the ends tied under her chin.

She said she thought little touches of femininity did wonders for a riding habit, that she considered most riding suits far too severe.

At the breakfast table that morning one of the dudes had suggested riding up the river to Eagle Creek, so everybody seemed surprised when Earl turned up Gunbarrel instead. He explained to me that night that he didn't have the courage to take her out where passing cars could see them. "I'll have to get used to it gradually," he said.

Her complaints about Badger began after the first ride, and I can't say I blamed her. He couldn't have been more exasperating, plugging along the trail behind the others, tree-brushing from side to side. Earl whispered in his ear when they stopped to rest and told him not to lay it on so thick, but Badger only shook his mane and ambled home at the same rate of speed. He wasn't so dumb—he knew that Earl would have to give her another horse. It had worked before and was worth trying again.

Next day she rode Pronto, who stepped up a little, but it didn't take him long to learn that here was a dude of whom he could take advantage. Soon he was meandering along as leisurely as Badger had done.

They were riding up the highway when she said, "I don't see why you don't give me a lively horse like the one you are riding. See how he throws his head up and steps right along, while Pronto hangs his down and I wear my legs out kicking him to keep up with you."

Earl was so tired of her complaining that he forgot all about being tactful.

"Why, Miss Lane, I happen to be riding Badger, the horse you called an old plug yesterday. Would you like him back?"

Patches was guiding the dudes the morning of her accident. They were riding slowly along the shoulder of a bare mountainside when he looked back to see her swing her leg around the saddle horn and ride on in that restful position. No doubt she had seen one of the cowboys do the same thing, but he warned her, saying, "You'd better not do that, Miss Lane. Pront's sensitive around the shoulders and might not like it."

Knowing all about horses, she didn't take much stock

Miss Lane, angry and humiliated, sprawled in the midst of boulders and prickly-pear cactus.

in his advice, and she delayed putting her foot back in her stirrup, carelessly rubbing against Pronto's neck in doing so.

Patches heard a commotion and looked back to see Miss Lane, angry and humiliated, sprawled in the midst of boulders and prickly-pear cactus. He knew she would never be able to ride home unless a "major operation" was performed. He laid her down across his lap and pulled the prickers from her seat, taking a fiendish delight in her every wince.

At the corral one morning, while waiting for the group to assemble, I witnessed an outstanding act of diplomacy. Among the swamp angels was one the cowboys called "Miss High Hat."

She complained about her horse; she said he didn't have enough life and she said she was quite capable of handling a faster animal. I wondered what could be done about it, having heard Earl say that all of the horses were being ridden.

To my surprise, Earl agreed with her and said pleasantly, "You wait here, Miss Jamison, and I'll see what I can find."

He led Socks back to the barn, and I edged around the corner and hurried after him. I'd never seen a cowboy pull a horse out of his hat and didn't want to miss the show.

Earl was unsaddling her horse as I entered. He looked at me and winked, "It isn't fair, sneakin' up on a feller like that," he said. "I might want to use the same tactics on you someday."

Then he ducked into the saddle shed and brought out a bright red Navajo saddle blanket, a different saddle, and a fancy bridle studded with glittering conchas.

"Reckon I'd rather lend a bridle than lose a dude."

He slipped the bit into the horse's mouth and added a martingale to the rigging. Then he combed out the mane and tail and gave him a quick rubdown with a torn gunny sack dipped in the water trough. He mounted, spurred old Socks as though he were coming out of chute Number 5 on Widowmaker at the rodeo, and rode the prancing horse out of the barn to the corner of the corral where Miss Jamison was waiting.

She was delighted and told him that this was exactly the kind of horse she wanted. Earl never batted an eye as he said, apologetically, "I hope you have no objection to the tie down, Miss Jamison. 'What-the-Hell' throws his head without it."

Truer words were never spoken than Ma Crouch's when she warned me, "Running a dude ranch is no mean job!"

CHAPTER XXVI

—and Roughnecks

WHEN WE WEREN'T being entertained by the antics of the dudes, our attention was focused on the oddities of the roughnecks, for they had their temperamental ways, too, especially the cooks.

All the jobs that had anything to do with riding or horses were filled by men whom Earl knew personally, for we didn't dare risk injury to a guest or mistreatment to a horse. Both were our bread and butter.

We received numerous inquiries from men wanting that kind of work, and even girls applied for jobs as wranglers. One of these, a young lady from New York, wrote, "I can sit on top of the corral fence and holler 'Yippee' as loud as any cowboy."

One man applying for a job said that he had graduated from a correspondence school in horsemanship and would, in his spare time and at no extra charge, teach Earl how to break and train horses. That made such a hit with Earl that he didn't even answer the letter.

Some of the applications were ridiculous, like the one from a youth in Pittsburgh who wrote:

Can you afford to keep me at your ranch for three years? If so, I will be the happiest young man alive.

My uncle, who lived in the West, made a fortune, and in his will he made a list of requirements for me to fulfill in three years. He wants me to work for a rancher, the wages to be based on my ability to work. If I fulfill his requirements I will be left his fortune; if not, it will go to charity. Since you know what I am up against, I hope you will give me a chance; but whether I fail or succeed, the rancher who tries to help me will receive many times the price he paid.

I was excited over the letter, but Earl smelled a mouse and wrote him that, while we regretted passing up such a golden opportunity, all the jobs for the summer were filled. I've often wondered if some less suspecting rancher took the bait.

It took three typewritten pages to list the qualifications of one couple who applied for work. Between them they had so many degrees that, had we hired them, I would never have had the nerve to ask the man to fill the wood box or his wife to make hot cakes. He even listed her favorite recipes, casserole dishes, Mexican specialties, frappés and hors d'oeuvres. Besides doing our gardening, bookkeeping, letter writing, cooking, wrangling, and entertaining, they said they would be happy to give instructions to our guests in Spanish, swimming, tennis and skiing—all this for a modest salary plus a welcome for their two small children. They guaranteed that the children wouldn't take any of their time that couldn't be spared from their jobs. "There are several ways of assuring this," he wrote. With only one toddler to watch, I was tempted to write and ask him for his formula; for every time a dude wanted me to do something, young Buckshot made a parallel demand on my time.

Rarely did a girl applying for a job as a waitress mention her ability to wait table, but all of them could ride horseback, loved the great out-of-doors, would adore entertaining the dudes for us, could play a guitar and sing, and were young and attractive.

When we were starting out, we fell for offers from Eastern boys who wanted to come out and work all summer for their board and room. It sounded economical, but the boys usually proved to be enormous eaters and disinterested workers.

The first of these were a couple of husky college athletes who looked strong enough to tackle any ranch job, so Earl set them to building a fence around the garden spot. He showed them how to dig the holes and tamp the posts with dirt and gravel. One of them claimed to have built fence before, and both said they would sure "do her up right." When Earl went out to stretch and staple the wire, the posts popped right out of their sockets, and he had to tamp them all again.

"Might as well have done the job myself," he grumbled.

In one instance, dude help turned out to be as satisfactory as professional help. A man and his son from New Jersey were guests at the ranch one summer; and during their stay we took a pack trip into the Jackson Hole country. They were two of the most enjoyable dudes we ever had. The lad was only seventeen, but he was a big strapping fellow; he never got in the way offering his services, but he was always in a handy spot when help was needed. The following spring his father wrote, asking if we would take him on for the summer for his board and room; and Earl decided to risk it. One morning soon after his arrival Earl sent him out to bring in the horses.

Fortunately we had only a few dudes at the time, and they were the type that weren't put out when ten o'clock came and there were no horses. When noon came and still no horses, Earl saddled Badger and went to see what was the matter. He tracked Doug for miles and finally found him sitting under a big pine tree, crying his eyes out. Earl said his first impulse was to laugh, but the boy looked so forlorn and frustrated that he didn't have the heart. Doug had been trying his hardest all morning to bunch the horses and bring them in. Failing, he had sat down under a tree to cry out his disappointment. After that, Earl took him out for several mornings and showed him how to wrangle. Doug caught on quickly and held the job all summer and turned out to be one of the best wranglers ever.

Expecting a new cook had much the same effect on me as setting fire under a balky mule.

Earl came into the kitchen the day before our first cook arrived to find me up to my neck in house cleaning.

"What's the idea?" he asked. "I thought the new cook was coming tomorrow. Why don't you let her clean the kitchen?"

"I'd pass out if she saw these dirty cupboards. Judging from what I hear about ranch cooks, she'd probably turn on her heel and stamp out of the kitchen if the place wasn't clean when she arrived."

The reports were not exaggerated. You had to be on your toes to keep a cook. We tried all kinds, but all of them were temperamental in one way or another.

Since we were booked up with pack trips that first summer, we advertised for a man and his wife; she was to cook at the ranch and he to go with the pack outfit, helping at the ranch between trips. A couple of days later a woman knocked at the kitchen door and inquired about the job. I supposed her husband had gone to the corral to see Earl, so I told her about her duties and was favorably impressed. I asked her if she wanted to go out and look at the tent house reserved for the cook.

When we stepped out the door, I was surprised to see a man sitting in the car.

"Couldn't you find my husband?" I called.

He only grunted and she answered for him, "He's scared to get out of the car. He's afraid of dogs."

I walked over to the car, where Ring was lying, amiably wagging a welcome.

"If you are looking for a job, you will find my husband out at the barn," I told him.

"Don't know as I am," he replied in a surly voice.

"Do you know how to drive a team?" I asked in embarrassment.

"Nope."

"Can you wrangle and pack horses?"

"First thing I'd do is get sick. Can't stand corral dust."

I gave up and turned to the woman.

"Well, I guess there's no point in showing you your room since your husband doesn't want the job."

She hopped into the car beside him and they rode off.

It must have been half an hour later when a second tap brought me to the kitchen door and I was surprised to see the same woman standing there. Embarrassed, she explained that her car was stuck halfway down the lane and asked if we would give it a push. I told her she'd have to wait until Earl came in.

"Where's your husband?"

"He's pulled out and left me," she answered blankly.

"Pulled out? Where?" I asked.

"He's gone to the highway to bum a ride to town."

"And left you alone with a broken-down car?" I was astonished.

"Oh," she excused him, "he's like that when things go wrong. Hasn't got no patience. He's been without work for over a month and his nerves is edgy. It ain't good for him to be without a job."

As soon as Earl got back, he helped start her car.

Three or four interviews followed before we found the right couple. We were sure that the Turners would fill the bill, for he was familiar with ranch and camp activities, and she was a neat, refined little woman who turned out to be an excellent cook, once I weaned her from banana flavoring.

I didn't dare come right out and say, "We don't like banana flavoring." I had learned that a policy of outspokenness was not the proper approach when one wanted to change the ways of a cook—not if she was worth keeping. Better delve into French history and employ some of the pet intrigues of Louis XIV. A mule skinner had an easier job, cajoling his Jack and Jenny.

When the flavor of banana appeared in the chocolate pie, I knew that something would have to be done. But what—and how? I first complimented her on the well-cooked roast and then remarked casually, "Mrs. Turner, that's the first time I ever tasted chocolate pie flavored with banana."

"Oh, is it?" she replied. "Chocolate pie is flat without it, I always say."

Hating myself for a moral coward, I conceded the

victory to her and left the kitchen feeling more like an imposter than the mistress of the house.

"If I can't win by fair means, I'll have to resort to foul," I told myself. When the door had closed behind her that evening, I pounced like a praying mantis on the bottle of banana flavoring and dumped it down the drain.

Next morning, when she asked about it, I explained with studied carelessness, "We popped corn last night, and I must have spilled it when I reached for the salt."

She ordered another bottle, and the flavor popped up in the mayonnaise in fruit salad. When several of the guests complained, I knew that something would have to be done—and quickly. No more shilly-shallying. I'd have to gird my armor and face the foe. I sallied to the kitchen, resolved to have it out once and for all; but when I stepped across the threshold, my legs went limp and I squeaked, "The funniest thing has happened, Mrs. Turner. I must be allergic to banana flavoring, for I've noticed that every time I taste it, I get sick. Maybe we had better change to vanilla."

"Oh, I'm sorry," she sympathized, "but there's no need to spoil things for the rest of us. Next time I bake, I'll save out a little of the dough and bake it separately for you."

Providentially, fate stepped in and solved the problem. She spilled the bottle and I got in cahoots with the groceryman, who sent word that he hadn't been able to get any banana flavoring.

It was while she was there that Earl stalked into our cabin one morning before going to town to get supplies.

"Haven't we got enough help in the kitchen?" he barked.

"Of course," I answered. "Why do you ask?"

"Well, when I stopped to get the grocery order, Mrs. Turner told me to bring back a new chore girl. Unless we get a lot more business, I don't see how we can afford extra help."

When I explained to him that a chore girl was a copper pot scraper, he shrugged his shoulders. "Well, I'll be darned! It's getting so nobody calls a spade a spade any more."

All went well in the kitchen until after the Fourth of July. Earl sent Mr. Turner out on a pack trip; and Mrs. Turner moved into the tent house with Denie, so we could use her cabin for dudes during the rush season.

Two days passed uneventfully; but on the third night, Denie was awakened by a flashlight flickering about the cabin. Mrs. Turner was kneeling over her suitcase; startled, she mumbled something about a handkerchief. Denie went back to sleep but a few hours later was again awakened. She could barely discern a figure stealing toward the suitcase but decided not to let Mrs. Turner know that she was awake.

Next morning Denie told us about Mrs. Turner's mysterious actions, and we conjured up a thriller, "The Riddle of the Locked Suitcase."

A few days after her husband left, we began to notice a change in Mrs. Turner. She grew careless about her cooking; her meals were often late; and she couldn't settle down to anything if Charlie was in the kitchen.

Charlie, our horse wrangler, was a confirmed bachelor; and as soon as he noticed Mrs. Turner's attraction to him, he stayed out of her way.

"I'm not gonna get mixed up in no triangle," he said.

Once she even tried swooning, making sure that Charlie was there to catch her. After that he was as wary as a coyote and ducked for cover every time she hove in sight.

I should have suspected her trouble the time I caught her tittering unnaturally and chasing Buckshot around the table.

The climax came when Denie rushed into our cabin before breakfast one morning to say that Mrs. Turner had gone completely berserk, that she was dancing around the kitchen and had put stove polish in the pancake batter. When Denie tried to stop her, she giggled and said, "It will add zip to the pancakes."

I dressed hurriedly and followed Denie to the kitchen where we persuaded Mrs. Turner to go to bed.

After breakfast Earl went to her cabin and found her sleeping soundly. She had left her suitcase open; and when he came back to the kitchen, he announced, "Well, the mystery is solved. Mrs. Turner's drunk. Has been more or less ever since Andy left. Her suitcase is full of dead soldiers."

"That's funny," I replied. "I've never smelled a thing on her breath but cloves."

He gave me a look that would have withered a cactus.

Her successor, Mrs. Sanders, was a Southerner and cooked with the lavish hand of one who doesn't have to pay the bills.

Disease was Mrs. Sanders' hobby. One look at a person and she could tell what ailed him, and something always did. A flushed face indicated a fever; a pallor, anemia; dark circles under the eyes could mean

but one thing, an ingrown goiter; a good appetite
was a good sign of worms; a poor one, the first symp-
tom of tuberculosis. According to her, nobody on
the ranch enjoyed good health. If she couldn't find
anything else the matter with us, she would tell by
the look in our eyes that some dreadful parasite was
"gnawin' at our vitals."

When I made the mistake of saying, "You certainly
look well this morning, Mrs. Sanders," she was insulted.

"Well, looks are deceivin'," she complained. "I ain't
never well. Fact is, sometimes I wonder how I keep
goin'—fragile as I feel most of the time."

The size of our ranch didn't warrant hiring more
than two women to help with the work, so we chose
a cook and a combination waitress and cabin girl. This
left the laundry and odd jobs for me. It didn't upset
the routine to have the hostess called away from the
tubs as much as it did from seven-minute icing or a
cheese omelet. Earl, Jr., took a lot of watching, and
I could keep him with me at the laundry. Besides, I
despised cooking for dudes. Even pinch-hitting between
cooks brought on a spell of temper. Cooking was
not only the hardest and most thankless job on the
ranch, but it also required the most concentration.
How could one concentrate with a dudine running
in to borrow a needle or a youngster demanding a
bandage on a cut finger?

Once I'd been pinch-hitting for a week when Earl
called from town to say that he had found a cook
and was bringing her right out. Mrs. McGuffy had
scarcely removed her hat before I pranced her to the
kitchen, showed her where things were kept, asked
her to stir up a spice cake for supper, and joyfully
slammed the door behind me.

About fifteen minutes before supper, I peeped into the kitchen and was surprised to see the batter for the cake still in the bowl.

"What happened? Why didn't you bake the cake?"

"You didn't ask me to bake it. You only said to stir it up," was her reply.

As it turned out, Mrs. McGuffy couldn't flex a muscle without instruction. She couldn't cook meat without a waterless cooker, couldn't knead bread because it gave her a backache, and didn't expect to wash dishes when she hired out as a cook.

The next morning I was back in the harness in a vile humor, and Earl was on his way to town to find another cook.

His was an easier job, taking care of the outside work. Cowboys were more plentiful than cooks.

And what cowboys! No wonder the dude girls fell in love with them; for even an ordinary man looks romantic decked out in a checked wool shirt, fancy-topped high-heeled boots, and a ten-gallon Stetson set at a rakish angle. And most of the dude wranglers were not ordinary-looking to start with. It was part of a wrangler's job to look nice, and they spent more money for clothes and an outfit than for anything else.

Patches was my favorite of all the cowboys who ever worked for us. He was seldom without a bandage, the result of his latest encounter with a bronc. There was never a maverick too wild or a bronco too snaky for him to try. He couldn't count his broken bones, and once a saddle horn had punctured one of his lungs.

Practical jokers are, as a rule, unpopular around dudes, but Patches was an exception. He was always up to something, but nobody ever got mad at him, at least not for long. None of his pranks was malicious

And what cowboys! No wonder the dudes fell in love with them

or too embarrassing. The humor of the situation was all that interested Patches.

One morning I was invited to join a party of dudes on a trip to the park. Having once had a transfusion of geyser blood, I never passed up an opportunity to visit Yellowstone.

As we approached Fishing Bridge and were inching our way through the crowds of fishermen—the old bridge had no sidewalk—we passed several triumphant anglers carrying long sticks of fish over their shoulders. At the end of the bridge just before the road widened, Patches leaned out of the car and grabbed a string of fish from one of the men, stepped on the gas, and hurried around the bend of the road. Before the trees shut off the view, we looked back to see the victim screaming angrily and waving his arms at the car.

We had scarcely caught our breath to register disapproval when the car approached another fisherman who hadn't been so fortunate and was leaving the river empty-handed. Patches leaned out of the car again and flung the string of fish at him, driving off as before. I never saw a man more astonished, but Patches only chuckled.

During twenty years of dude wrangling, I don't suppose we had over eight or ten complaints about the help; and most of them were from lovesick dudines who felt that they weren't getting their share of the wranglers' attention.

Some of the wranglers were as mercenary as any gold digger. One Casanova celebrated his birthday soon after the arrival of each new bunch of dudes. By the end of the summer he was well supplied with haberdashery bearing such swanky trade names as Lord and Taylor, Marshall Field, and Bonwit Teller.

When newly arrived Miss Hicks announced, "Now don't you go to a big lot of trouble for me; just let me browse around and entertain myself," we knew that here was a dudine who would want her Western hospitality broiled and served in paper lace panties. Just for the fun of it, we let her "browse around by herself."

Of course it didn't work, and she grew more demanding every day. When she came to the breakfast table early one morning and tapped her glass with a teaspoon for service, Denie had all she could take and promptly told her off. Miss Hicks came running to me.

"I won't be exposed to such insolence again. Either Miss Denie or I will have to leave. Why, do you know, she got up early this morning to ride with the wrangler and came to the kitchen late, reeking, simply reeking, of the stable."

That night I told Earl about it. "Earl, I hate to say anything to Denie, but I'll have to do something. What shall I tell her?"

"Tell Denie?" he questioned. "Why tell her anything? Miss Hicks is the one who ought to be told; and while you're doing it, you can tell her that if she don't like good, clean horse smell, she's in the wrong stall."

CHAPTER XXVII

Pack Trips Are Fun

TIME PASSED so rapidly that summer, my first as mistress of Gunbarrel. The last pack trip before the hunting season was to leave on the tenth of August for Cooke City and Grasshopper Glacier. The new guests from Vermont, Mr. and Mrs. Howard and their two children, were to arrive Saturday afternoon and start their two-weeks trip Sunday morning.

Nobody went riding that Saturday morning—the dudes were all too interested in the activity around the storehouse, where Earl and Shorty, the horse wrangler, were getting ready for the trip. I had helped several times before, but never with more interest than now —and with good reason. On the previous afternoon Earl had burst into the cabin where Denie and I were playing with the baby and announced, "Jim's quit, without giving me any notice, and I'm in one hell of a fix. Where I'll find a trail cook at this late hour is more than I know."

"You really are in trouble," I agreed. "If it weren't for the baby, I'd offer to take the job myself, but I guess that's out."

"How come?" Denie chimed in. "I thought I was

a sharecropper in this outfit! I don't see why you can't leave Buckshot with me for a couple of weeks. With Patches here to look after the dudes, Dollie in the kitchen, and the road open in case of emergencies, I'm not afraid to tackle it. It would be fun!" Denie was like that—whenever she did a favor, she'd switch it around to make herself the receiver rather than the giver.

And so another wish was coming true. I was going on my first pack trip, even if it was as the cook. That meant falling off my horse and peeling potatoes the minute we stopped for the night. Much as I disliked cooking, it would be worth it!

Earl kept a list of necessary items tacked to the wall of the storehouse and checked each as he put it into a pannier. (Panniers are boxes which fit on the sides of pack saddles.) Besides canned goods, dried fruit, flour, sugar, and other staples, the list included fresh meat and, of all things, yeast and spices. Surely they couldn't expect to bake bread over a campfire! The camp cookstove with its detachable oven was the answer. It was made of sheet iron and fitted into a set of panniers, the removable stove legs and stovepipe having first been wrapped in burlap and put into the firebox. It cooked and baked almost as good as Virginia, so camping didn't mean eating out of tin cans or simply frying potatoes and bacon over a campfire. Many treats came out of that oven, including fresh yeast rolls, pie, cake, and, of course, biscuits.

We had chairs and tables, too. The canvas table tops had wooden slats sewed into them like stays in a corset, and these were fastened over a set of collapsible legs when in use. When packed, the legs folded into a compact bundle, the top rolled up scrollwise, and both fitted into a canvas bag. The chairs were built on the same principle. The dudes generally brought their own sleeping bags and air mattresses with them. When Denie saw Earl put a bicycle pump in the pack, she inquired, "What are you putting that in for? I thought horses wore iron shoes."

"Ever since I took seven swamp angels out for a ten-day pack trip, I've carried this. Blowing up seven air mattresses by mouth every night is no picnic."

Other standard articles were candles, toilet paper, horseshoe tools and nails, a first-aid kit, sewing items, playing cards, and a saw, pick, and shovel.

The panniers were packed two at a time to balance the load, the packer hefting each article to make sure they were of equal weight. A full pannier weighs about fifty or sixty pounds. Most of ours were home-made of hardwood and a little narrower than an apple box. They were covered with rawhide or canvas to make them stronger and easier to handle, and often reinforced with iron bands. All except those containing the fresh food and the dudes' personal belongings were packed that Saturday to get us off to an earlier start next morning.

On Sunday the men wrangled the horses at daybreak, then saddled the pack horses and tied them to hitching racks so they could be loaded after breakfast. The wooden saddles had a special construction, resembling a sawbuck without legs. A thick saddle pad protected the horse's back.

To pack a horse, Earl stood on one side of the animal and Shorty on the other, each hanging a pannier to the packsaddle forks with loops of the same rope and pulling it taut. Such articles as the camp chairs and tables were then laid lengthwise in the forks of the

Then all was covered with a canvas pack cover and securely roped with a diamond hitch.

sawbuck, and a bulky article like a sleeping bag or tent was folded on top. Then all this was covered with a canvas pack cover and the entire load was securely roped with a diamond hitch, a series of trick loops and knots which formed a small diamond on the top of the pack and made the load fast, no matter how rough the country or how jolting the horse's gait. Roany, the most dependable pack horse and the one with the easiest gait, always carried the eggs, each of which was paper-wrapped and carried in a tin box kept for that purpose.

In some localities the first pack horse is led by the guide, and the second is tied by its halter rope to the looped-up tail of the first, and so on down the line. In our country, however, the horses were taught to follow the guide single file, the halter ropes fastened to rings on the side of the saddle. Each horse knew its proper place in the line and fought for it, if necessary.

When the horses were packed, Earl and Shorty adjusted the dudes' saddle stirrups to a comfortable length and rolled their lunches in their slickers and tied them by the saddle strings to the backs of their saddles. With Earl in the lead, we were on our way, and the pack horses fell naturally into their places behind him. Shorty rode next, then the dudes, and I brought up the rear. As I looked back and saw my son waving good-by from Denie's arms, I swallowed hard. Two weeks was a long time to be separated from a seven-months-old baby.

In order to reach the turnoff that led to Cooke City, we traveled for several miles along a trail beside the main road. When it cut into a dugway, we had to take the same route as the automobiles. Most drivers were considerate and slowed down when they saw riders approaching, but sometimes a driver took delight in sneaking up behind and honking his horn just to see the horses jump and to startle the riders. Several times I've seen Earl stop his horse in the middle of the road, halt an approaching car, and request the driver to slow up or stop blowing his horn. That's why we never took dudes riding on the highway unless absolutely necessary.

That morning we were stopped twice by tourists who wanted to take our pictures. Although it slowed us up, Earl always obliged, and when I asked him why, he explained, "You never can tell when one of those pictures will be an ad for your place. One of Timber Lodge's best customers first heard of the ranch when he stopped to take a picture of their outfit going down the road."

The first day out was uneventful to the rest of the crew; but to me it was adventure merely to ride in the procession. I feasted on the magnificent scenery and delighted in the reactions of the dudes and horses to the sounds, sights, and smells of the forest.

Every pack string has at least one tree brusher, and Popcorn was the culprit in ours. As he walked along, he would eye first one side of the trail and then the other, until, spying two trees growing side by side without enough room between them for easy passage, he would deliberately step off the trail and consider the possibilities. Pleased with his choice, he would wiggle-waggle through the space and loosen the pack as though he were saying, "You put this pack on me; now I'll make you work to keep it there." Sure enough, one of the men would have to dismount and pull the ropes taut again.

Among our pack animals we had one mule we called

Kate. She was the smartest animal we ever had on the place. She knew that she was teacher's pet and took advantage of her position at every opportunity. She always led the pack horses and would bite any who disputed her position. If her pack ever slipped or came loose, she would stop dead still in the middle of the trail. No matter how hard the animals behind egged her on, she wouldn't budge until one of the men made things right. Then, smug and self-satisfied, she would sail on down the trail.

The Howards were nice people, interested and eager, although Mr. Howard was impatient and inclined to be bossy. Earl listened to all his suggestions, then did as he pleased. Mr. Howard was always picking out a "better camp site." Several times his Boy Scout son came to the rescue by saying, "Dad, can't you see that there isn't any water there?" or "Where would we get wood if we stopped here?"

Contrary to opinion, scenery and water are not the prime requisites for a camp site. We passed up some seemingly lovely places for others not half as nice, I thought; but when I spoke of it to Earl, he said, "There's much more to a camp site than water and looks—dry wood, for instance, and, above all, pasture for the horses. The ideal location is at the edge of a dense forest, where there's slim pickin's on the home side of us, and good pasture in the direction we're headed for. The horses aren't so apt to take off for home that way."

Some friends had offered us the use of their cow camp, so we didn't need to worry about a spot that first night; but no twenty-four hours on a pack trip passes without incident. When we stopped, Mr. Howard volunteered to help unpack.

"Sure," Earl said, "you can start on Roany."

Mr. Howard untied the diamond hitch and the next thing we knew the horse was bucking for the trees and scattering eggs "from hell to breakfast." Poor Mr. Howard! He had neglected to tie the horse, and the falling pack cover had spooked Roany.

The prospect of no eggs for the rest of the trip was appalling; but with one taste of the remaining few we scrambled for supper, we not only forgave but blessed both Roany and Mr. Howard. Those eggs were anything but fresh!

We didn't rough it that night. We slept on straw mattresses in the bunk beds! Neither the dudes nor I had ever been in a cow camp before, so we enjoyed the experience and imagined we could hear the strains of "Git along, little dogies" reverberating through the log walls.

When morning dawned, clear as mountain water, we ate a ravenous breakfast—nobody even missed eggs. Shorty was the only one absent as he hadn't come in yet with the horses. With the dudes, I never ceased to marvel at the ability of the wrangler to gather the horses in strange country and bring them in to the rope corral every morning. When he wasn't familiar with the lay of the land, he would get up in the middle of the night to follow a horse bell if he thought it was moving too rapidly out of earshot. In any event, he was always the first one up—and the only one in camp who could be late for breakfast without getting a ribbing.

En route to Crandall Creek Ranger Station that day, Mrs. Howard suffered her most embarrassing moment.

We stopped for lunch in a sunny, inviting clearing beside a small stream, its banks lush with ferns and wild flowers. After dinner, Mrs. Howard took to the bushes to avoid stopping the procession later in the afternoon.

Suddenly the horses began to snort and whinny.

"Wonder what ails those fool horses," Earl said.

The words were scarcely uttered when we heard something charging through the underbrush. My first thought was "It's a bear, and he's headed in our direction!" and I dashed to Earl's side. A moment later we saw the source of the commotion. It was Mrs. Howard, lunging from the bushes, eyes like saucers, her riding trousers halfway between her knees and her waist.

"Help! A bear!" she gasped as she stumbled up to us.

Not until she was safe did she realize the ludicrous picture she made—and only then did she begin grabbing frantically for her trousers. She was so embarrassed she hardly looked up from her saddle horn the rest of the afternoon, and her husband didn't help matters any by kidding her unmercifully about being frightened out of her senses—and her riding pants.

We laid over for a day at a delightful camp site where Crandall Creek emptied into the Clarks Fork River. While Mr. Howard and Earl fished and the cook went marketing, Mrs. Howard and the children enjoyed a lazy day floating down the river on inflated air mattresses and sun bathing on the clean sandy shore. I came home with a "mess o' potherbs" for supper and enough wild strawberries for a shortcake. With the fish the men caught, we had a wonderful dinner, courtesy of Mother Nature.

A layover was an excuse to play at housekeeping, stacking up the panniers to look like cupboards and arranging the camp dishes and supplies in an orderly fashion. It meant washing up the dish and face towels, cooking something special for supper, or maybe baking cookies for the next day's lunch; but most of all it meant that I had time to roam the inviting trails near camp, search for new wild flowers, and drink in the wonder of it all.

Riding along a mountain trail through rock-studded, forest-dotted country during the day and camping near a fish-laden stream or lake in the early evening creates an awareness of nature you don't get from any other experience. To go to sleep with the sound of water hurrying past the camp and soft winds sighing through the needled boughs is to awaken next morning completely refreshed. For a taste of the real West, there is nothing like a pack trip!

CHAPTER XXVIII

Cooke City

WHEN WE learned that a new highway was to be built through the virgin wilderness between Red Lodge and Cooke City, Montana, all the ranchers in the vicinity were incensed. We considered Cooke City our private "last frontier" and resented every auto track left on its soft-padded streets, every filling station constructed on ground consecrated to hitching racks.

It was a selfish viewpoint, for only a privileged few ever saw the beauty of the Beartooth Mountains before the highway linked them with other roads. We argued that, since the road could be kept open only for two or three months out of the year, it wouldn't attract enough travel to warrant the expense of building it. Besides, there were already four automobile entrances to Yellowstone Park, and wasn't that enough without spoiling our horse and buggy road!

Only last summer we drove through Cooke City in a car, and I couldn't resist a longing to see it again as it was the first time I rode down the main street with the Howards behind a string of pack horses.

It was just a dirt road then, and there weren't enough vehicles passing over it to keep the grass down. The

town, a collection of hillsides, had once hummed with
the activity of prospectors attracted by the gold in
"them thar hills." All of the buildings were very old,
many of them abandoned. Sun and storm had weathered
the old, unfinished logs to a silver gray that looked as
familiar to the hillsides as the rocks and trees that
lived there. Behind the town were tall, rugged, pictur-
esque mountains, pitted with old diggings and laced
with the trails of prospectors long gone. Fir and pine
trees grew in careless abandon.

Including the hermits, placer miners, and trappers,
there weren't more than forty people living in the
community; and the average age of these was well over
sixty. It was not an uncommon sight to see two long
beards standing on the corner with a plug of chewing
tobacco between them. One of them would be saying to the other, "Wall, I won't take a cent less'n
fifty thousand fer my claim." They were discussing
what they would do on that fabulous day when the
railroad came through Cooke.

At the time, before the highway was built, the arrival of a pack train created a sensation in the town
and everybody came out to see it.

Cooke City boasted one general store, and part of
it was given over to the post office. The Metropolitan
Hotel still functioned and was operated by the same
people who built it in 1880 during the boom days.
Having made the trip many times before, Earl knew
most of the old-timers and introduced us to the characters of the town.

The hotel and its proprietors fascinated us most. The
Adamses were a refreshing couple. He was a dapper
little man of eighty who wore a black and white pin-
checked suit, gaiters, a worn celluloid collar and frayed

black bow tie. His little round chin-whiskered face set down in the collar like a ball in a socket. The elbows and neck of his coat and the seat of his pants were almost threadbare, and there was a grim "lived in a long time" look about his suit; but he wore his clothes with pride, a gentleman born.

His wife was outstanding, too. A gay person, she had been reluctant to part with youth and had only recently given up dyeing her hair. Near the roots it was silky and white; then there was a streak of henna which frizzed out into dark ends. The hem of her dress was uneven and struck her legs about an inch above her high-buttoned shoes. The folds of long underwear showed through her cotton stockings and made little puffs. But her eyes and complexion caught your gaze. Her eyes were a bright azure, reflecting interest in everything; and her skin was like a baby's —even the wrinkles had a smooth texture.

She led us on a tour of the hotel. We were intrigued with the old building which bent a little here, bulged a bit there, and leaned in first one direction and then another. It was a paradox of beautiful furniture and ugly backgrounds. Some of the stringers underneath the floor had rotted, so walking across it gave you the same rolling sensation as that of a ship on a rough sea. The stairs wobbled as we climbed them. The treads were carpeted with hand-hooked rugs, well worn but still beautiful. All of the bedrooms were furnished much the same: a fancy iron bed, oak dresser, center table; an old-fashioned commode, a china washbowl, pitcher, and soap dish on top, and below, in a cubbyhole, a pot, the lid covered with a crocheted husher. Everywhere were lovely hooked rugs, each done in a different design.

Including the hermits, placer miners, and trappers there weren't more than forty people living in the community.

Several of the bedrooms were papered with old newspapers, and on one I noticed the date 1901. Mrs. Adams apologized for the tattered condition of this room.

"We haven't gotten around to papering it for several years." This was in 1924.

The back stairs were even more hazardous than the front ones, and we heaved sighs of relief when we stepped into the dining room. Two tables were spread with once-white cotton tablecloths, bespeckled now with egg yolk and coffee stains. In one end of the room stood an old-fashioned square piano, encased in beautiful hand-carved mahogany. She proudly told us that it had been packed in by mule train and assembled in this very room. She sat down at the piano and said, "Now, you young'uns dance a waltz while I play. I can play waltzes real well."

She began "Over the Waves," and I recalled the last time I danced to that tune, only now it was the floor and not my partner who provided the rough sea. The piano hadn't been tuned for years. The discord was terrific and, to make matters worse, the loud pedal stuck. We didn't dare look at each other as we danced for fear we'd burst into laughter.

Our next stop was in the old bar. It contained a conglomeration of odd-shaped and glittering rocks, pieces of board, broken stools and showcases, a few old antiques, and several trunks. She opened one of these to take out some old shawls and dresses. It was like a peek into an antiquated copy of *Godey's Lady's Book*.

Among the rubble Mrs. Howard spied a pair of silver cocktail shakers and asked her if she would consider selling them.

"They are no good to us any more," the little old

lady said. "You can have them if you want them, for a keepsake." Mrs. Howard tucked a ten-dollar bill in Mrs. Adams' pocket.

In the meantime her husband was talking to Earl in a corner of the lobby, asking him the familiar question, "Have you heard tell any more on the outside about when the railroad will be in Cooke?" The old-timers had never given up the hope that someday they would have transportation to a smelter for their ore, and this would bring good times to the town again. There was something pathetic about their persistent questioning.

The dudes got a bang out of the sheriff's office—a one-room log cabin with a big tin star nailed prominently over the door. They had to bend almost double to follow the sheriff, another octogenarian, into the low-ceilinged room, where they plied him with questions. We learned that there had been only three pupils enrolled in school the year before. He said the winters were bad, that all livestock was taken to the lower country early in the fall, and that nobody could venture out after Thanksgiving without skis or snowshoes. When an old prospector died in midwinter, the snow was so deep and the ground so hard that they couldn't dig a grave for him, so they kept the coffin containing the frozen corpse buried in a snowbank until spring.

As we rode back to camp late that afternoon, I overheard Mr. Howard say, "Today's experience is worth the price of the whole trip to me. I wouldn't have missed it for anything."

That night we pulled our bed out of the tent and slept under the stars. As we lay there listening to the tinkling music of the horse bells floating over the meadow, I whispered to Earl, "It's fun to make your living showing people like the Howards a good time, furnishing memories for them. A vacation that has been enjoyed is never forgotten."

"I guess you're right," he agreed sleepily. "Dude wranglin's not such a bad deal after all." Then he nudged me and added, " 'Specially when a fellow has a pinch-hitting wife for a side-kick," and fell off to sleep.

I lay awake for a long time enjoying the best compliment I had ever received from my husband.

CHAPTER XXIX

Rain, Rain, Go Away

IT WAS SPRINKLING when the dudes awoke next morning, enough to mark the ground with scattered wrinkles. Fortunately we were up and had moved our bedroll into the cook tent before it started. Since a trip to Grasshopper Glacier was slated for the day, we were disappointed about the weather and held a little pow-wow at breakfast to decide whether or not to go. Finally we left it up to Mr. Howard.

"If we go and it pours down rain, we'll soon forget how wet we got, but if we don't go and it clears up, we'll kick ourselves all winter for having been so close to the glacier without seeing it. I guess we might as well put on our slickers and get going."

I packed paper-sack lunches for all of us except Shorty, the horse wrangler, who stayed home by the fire.

"If you ask me," he said, "you're plumb loco starting out on a day like this. If it's raining here, it's pouring up there, or mebbe snowing. I'd rather stay down here and take to shelter along with the live grasshoppers than to ride twenty-eight miles in the rain jest to see a bunch of dead ones."

At first we enjoyed riding in the shower, the big raindrops spattering against our hats and slickers. That was while it came straight down and didn't hit us at right angles. When the trail narrowed and passed through a dense forest of second-growth trees, it became disagreeable. The water clung to the branches as we brushed through and seemed to come from all directions, rivering down our hatbrims, funneling down our necks, and dripping into our boot tops.

At an old abandoned smelter we dismounted to shake ourselves off. There was an old stove still set up, and unconsciously we reached out our cold hands, expecting warmth. Through a crack in the roof, Mr. Howard spied a patch of blue sky and optimistically prophesied that it would clear up in a little while.

When we resumed our ride and were picking our way through a clearing in which hacked-off tree stumps still stood, Badger got his foot caught in a piece of old wire and started kicking up his heels and cavorting around in his effort to get loose. In the shuffle I lost a stirrup and, afraid that I might be thrown against one of the sharp edges of a stump, picked a bare space and threw myself off, landing safely on a bare patch of ground. As I got to my feet, pleased with myself, it was only to hear Earl shout back at me, "My God, woman, what do you think you're doing?"

Surprised, I explained why I had jumped, but he only answered crossly, "Well, after this stay on your horse. You might have been killed."

My mouth opened to make some sarcastic retort, but shut again as I thought, "I guess he's right. Supposing I had been hurt—what a predicament! Nobody could have seen the glacier; the pack trip would have

The water clung to the branches as we brushed through and seemed to come from all directions.

broken up; and the dudes would have gone home disappointed—to say nothing of our financial loss!

Common sense had crooked its trigger finger and scored another bull's-eye!

Now and then the rain would peter out and the skies clear a little, enough to renew our hope, and then it would pour down harder than ever.

At noon we reached the timber line and the end of the horse trail. The rest of the way would be taken afoot. Here, on the side of a bare-faced stony mountain, stood a long hitching rack and a four-holed toilet, with a sign nailed over the doorless opening on which some wayfarer had printed the words, "Last Stop."

As we dismounted and led our horses up to the rack, the heavens opened up and the rain came down in sheets, literally digging holes in the ground. Earl tested the hitches to make sure the horses were fast, for by this time the boom of the thunder had turned to cracking, and loud echoes were reverberating through the air as if the mountains had fallen out and were arguing back and forth with gigantic voices. It was no wonder the horses were frightened.

Since there was no other shelter, not even a tree or bush, we all rushed into the Last Stop, where we found a door leaning against the wall. The men set it up at the opening and stood holding it there, while the rest of us pulled the lids over the holes and sat down in a huddle trying to dodge the deluge of water which poured through the cracks in the roof.

Somebody said, "Gee, I'm hungry. Let's eat." And Earl added, "We might as well. This is probably the only shelter we'll find."

As we opened our lunch sacks, we looked at each

other and all of us, even Earl, burst out laughing. What a picture we must have made!

"Well, I never thought I'd live to see the day when you'd be dining in such a swanky place as this, my dear," Mr. Howard said to his wife. "And don't think I'm going to keep it a secret when we get back home! You'll probably have to resign from the Garden Club once this bit of scandal leaks out."

It was over an hour before the storm let up enough for us to venture out and make our sorry way over the top of the mountain to the glacier, which lies cradled between Iceberg Peak and Mount Wilse. The wind blew so hard we could hardly stand on our feet; and the rain, which had taken all day to turn into a sleet, pelted our necks and faces.

Once over the top, the sight which met our eyes was almost unbelievable—an eighty-foot cliff of ice, the face of which was marked by black bands of frozen grasshoppers. The deepest band must have been at least sixty feet below the surface of the glacier.

Guide-wise, Earl explained the phenomenon.

"The story is that once during an epidemic of grass-hoppers, great swarms of them were carried by the wind to this great height. Passing over the glacier, they got cold and fell down. Fresh snow covered them and the process was repeated. Maybe years passed before the next ones were caught, as you'll notice that the bands aren't evenly spaced."

We picked out some hoppers, which were perfectly preserved, to take home with us to prove that we had actually been there.

When we returned to our horses, our one thought was to get back to camp, so the homeward trail seemed endless. One couldn't possibly imagine a wearier or

more woebegone procession than the one which trooped
into camp late that evening. It was still raining and
we were dripping wet, but the sight of smoke coming
from the camp cook tent revived our spirits. After
we had dried off and warmed up a little, we ate like
famished wolves and consumed quarts of coffee. We
had to admit that we were glad Shorty hadn't gone
along. I know I could never have cooked a meal that
night. After dinner the dudes retired at once, and
as soon as the dishes were washed, Earl and I gratefully
followed suit.

It was tough having to pack in the rain next morning. The gear was sodden and heavy and, even worse,
we knew we'd have to set up a wet camp that night.
All day it drizzled, but not a peep of complaint did
we hear from the Howards. When I spoke of it to
Mrs. Howard, she said, "Well, I guess none of us like
it, but we have to take the bitter with the sweet. It
will clear up tomorrow."

But tomorrow came and still it rained and by that
time we had reached the saturation point. Fortunately,
the beds had kept dry, that is, all of them except
ours. There must have been a weak spot in one of
the pack covers, for the rain had leaked through leaving a wet place in the middle of our bed as big as a
pancake griddle. I had supposed it would be impossible to sleep in a wet bed, but I soon discovered that
it could be done, and with comfort. Once we warmed
the wet spot with body heat, we slept like children.
It was getting in that was hard, like that first plunge
into an icy river.

On the third afternoon the skies cleared; and we
set up camp early, declaring a thanksgiving. Earl built
a huge bonfire in front of the cook tent and tied pack

ropes to trees close by. Over these we spread out all the beds, ours to dry and the others to air. After a big supper—mulligan stew with ham—we sat around the campfire until late, visiting, singing, and watching the firelight play upon the trees, the creek, and the tepees. Even after the others had left the fire and gone to bed, Earl and I sat there waiting for the last trace of dampness to evaporate from our blankets. As we snuggled down between the warm, dry flannel sheets, Earl said, "A feller can't possibly appreciate a dry bed if he has never slept in a wet one."

Hoping to run into the wild herd of buffalo which ranged along the Lamar River, we cut across the northeast corner of Yellowstone Park on our way home. Luck was with us, for we not only saw the buffalo but our view of them might well have been the setting of a Charles Russell painting. After crossing a high mesa, we were picking our way along the dim trail down a limestone rimrock when we discovered them grazing contentedly below us on either side of the river which flowed quietly through a long meadow. Accustomed as we were to seeing wild game, we were thrilled to the marrow and could easily imagine how much the dudes were enjoying the tableau stretched out before us as if painted on canvas.

On that trip we saw, besides the buffalo, a herd of elk and another of antelope, several deer, four mountain sheep, a couple of moose, a lone coyote—and, of course, Mrs. Howard's bear.

Earl was always the first to see the wild game in the forest. Camouflaged against a background of tree, rock, and shrub, an animal could be right ahead of me and I'd never see it.

When he called our attention to a coyote which

stood beside a tall sagebrush some distance away, Mrs. Howard saw it before I did and tossed a remark over her shoulder.

"I can't tell whether it's a coyote or a fox. Quite a fur piece, isn't it?"

"Why, yes," I answered, thinking her remark a little strange, "it would make a nice fur piece."

"Oh, I didn't mean that," she called back merrily. "You see, I was raised in Arkansas where anything far away is referred to as being 'a fur piece.'"

I made a mental note to remember that one for Denie to add to her collection. She had been gathering expressions all summer and incorporating them in her slang vocabulary. She "rode the fence" with the cowboy from Wyoming, "sat on the sofer" with the professor from New York, and, mimicking the lady from Boston, referred to the pine needles falling on the roof of her cabin as "spills."

We were only two days' ride from home when we ran into the moose yard. We noticed, as we passed through a willow thicket, that beaten trails turned off at all angles, separating it into little rooms, and that the bark on most of the saplings had been eaten off.

"That's what we call a moose yard," Earl told us. "That's where the family lives in winter."

"Just like people!" Mrs. Howard exclaimed in surprise.

"Yes," he went on, "they behave more like human bein's than any of the other animals in the forest. A bull moose keeps the same mate until she dies, and the parents take care of their young until they are almost full grown. It's not uncommon to see a bull and cow moose with a long yearling and a new calf together. They're browsing animals and live on leaves and bark rather than on grass, as elk do. In summer, leaves are their main food; and I've seen a bull hook his horns over a branch and bend it down so the family could eat. In winter, they pick a promisin' willow or alder thicket and, when the snows come, tramp down lanes so all the trees can be easily reached."

As we drew nearer home, I could hardly wait to get there, wondering how much the baby had grown since I had left and if he'd know me when I returned. It was disappointing when, on what was to be our last day out, Shorty couldn't find the horses until almost noon, and we didn't get started until after lunch.

It was sundown before we reached the river and Earl suggested, "I'll pull in at Old Tex's with the outfit and, after supper, I'll ride to the nearest telephone, call the ranch, and ask them to send the car up for you and the dudes. Shorty and I can bring the outfit home tomorrow."

I thought it a wonderful idea, but Mr. Howard protested.

"Nothing doing. We left the ranch horseback, and we're returning the same way."

"In that case," Earl said, "we'll set up camp at Old Tex's and be home for dinner tomorrow."

So we camped that night in the trees behind Old Tex's cabin, and after supper we spent a long evening visiting with him in his bachelor kitchen. He was in one of his yarning moods, and the dudes were captivated.

I couldn't help noticing the difference in his attitude toward me. It wasn't anything he said; it was just the way he included me in the conversation, as if I'd never even been a dude but had lived on the river always. It made me warm with gratitude.

CHAPTER XXX

Inventory

"How quiet it seems," I mused as I sat knitting in the living room before an open fire two weeks later, "but it's a nice kind of quiet, not the least bit lonely."

Dude season was over and hunting season had not yet begun; Earl had ridden down the river on an errand; the guests had all gone home; Dollie, the cook, had left for the winter; and Denie had accepted a teaching position in town. Only Earl, Jr., and I were left in the house, and he was sleeping in the little pole crib Earl had made for him.

It was a perfect afternoon for reminiscing, for thinking back over the past summer and checking the mistakes we'd made, the practices which had clicked and should be repeated another year. I must remember to tell the Howards when I wrote them that Earl had said they were the best sports he had ever guided on a pack trip—that was the kind of compliment that bore repeating. I must buy a little notebook and jot down the birthdays and the likes and dislikes of some of the guests. True, many of them would never return, but some of them would be back, if not next summer, another year. It would be fun to have lemon

"How quiet it seems," I mused as I sat knitting before the open fire

slices for Mrs. Taylor's tea, or pour the cream in Mrs. Hansen's cup first, because she liked her coffee better that way. Just little gestures, but often they were more important than the big ones.

And then I was startled out of my reverie by the ringing of the telephone. Lifting the receiver, I heard the voice of one of our down-country neighbors saying, "Do you folks plan on coming to the schoolhouse dance Saturday night?"

"We hadn't heard about it yet," I answered, "but if there is going to be one, I imagine we'll be there. Earl never misses a dance if he can help it."

"In that case, after the dance will you serve on the cleanup committee?" She continued, "I know it's a dirty job, but we thought you wouldn't mind."

Mind? Her request was like giving me a present! One didn't ask a person to scrub floors or empty ash trays unless they were friends—unless they belonged!

"I wonder why this sudden change of heart," I thought. "I've scarcely seen any of them all summer."

I could hardly wait for Earl to come home so I could tell him the good news. I related the telephone conversation word for word and added, "Earl, do you realize what this means?"

"Sure," he answered, "it means we'll lose another hour's sleep after the dance. I don't see why they can't ask somebody who lives closer to clean the schoolhouse."

"Why, Earl, how can you say that?" I protested. "It's wonderful! It means I'm one of you at last. Now why do you suppose they ever asked me to serve on the committee?"

"Oh, for a number of reasons, I suppose," he answered. "Like staying alone that night last winter;

like cooking for the outfit when Jim quit; like giving my grub-liner friends a handout when they stop in at all hours. News like that gets around, honey. I guess I can't call you my little half-breed any longer. You're just a common, everyday roughneck along with the rest of us now."

But had I, after all, changed so much? I was as curious as ever, only now I found out what I wanted to know by keeping my eyes and ears open instead of asking so many questions. Impetuous? Guilty again, but now I sifted and measured before adding. Talkative? Well, I had improved considerably in that respect, having discovered that people listen more attentively when the trivial and unimportant is left out of the conversation.

Long after Earl left the room, I sat there thinking, reviewing the happenings of the past two years, the richest in what was to be a long and satisfying life. They had been bountiful years in which I had acquired a husband, a son, and a home, and learned more lessons than I had ever learned in school; years which had taught me that one's life can be full of riches without owning stick or stone, that lack of fortune could make one poor in the "riches of the pocket" but could not lay hand on the riches of the mind and soul; years in which I had learned to pit my energies against misfortune and come out the victor, that had taught me the meaning of the word "neighbor."

And to think the answer was so simple! I hadn't seen the forest for the trees. Nothing difficult at all —just learning a few down-to-earth lessons which were bound to enrich the years that lay ahead—lessons that I might have learned months ago had I not been so carried away with my own importance.

And this was only the beginning, the first rung on the ladder. Now, there would be more demands upon my time and talent. More responsibility would mean less liberty. A reputation was one thing, living up to it another. But nothing could faze me now. Oh, it was good to be alive—and needed!

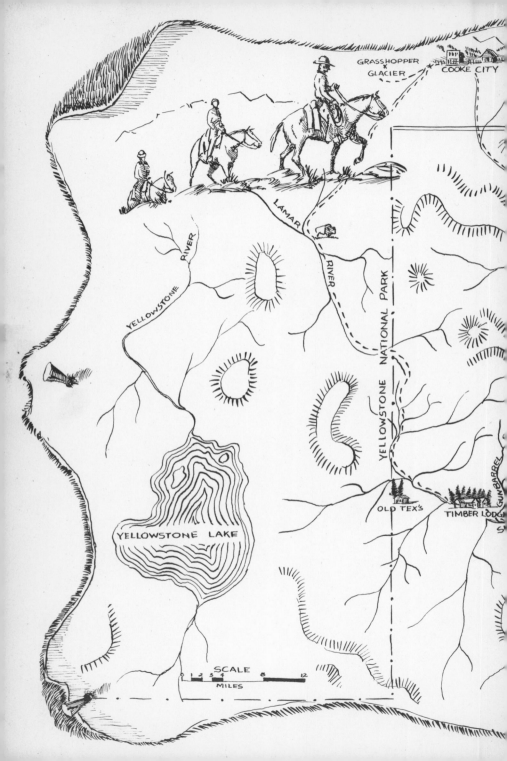

GRASSHOPPER
GLACIER

COOKE CITY

LAMAR

RIVER

YELLOWSTONE

RIVER

YELLOWSTONE NATIONAL PARK

YELLOWSTONE LAKE

OLD TEX'S

TIMBER LODGE

GUNBARREL

S.

SCALE

0 1 2 3 4   8   12

MILES